The Saxon Mars and his Force

The Saxon Army during the Reign of
John George III 1680–1691

Alexander Querengässer

Helion & Company

The Series Editor would like to thank Michal Paradowski for his help with sourcing images for the book.

Helion & Company Limited
Unit 8 Amherst Business Centre
Budbrooke Road
Warwick
CV34 5WE
England
Tel. 01926 499 619
Email: info@helion.co.uk
Website: www.helion.co.uk
Twitter: @helionbooks

Published by Helion & Company 2019
Designed and typeset by Mach 3 Solutions Ltd (www.mach3solutions.co.uk)
Cover designed by Paul Hewitt, Battlefield Design (www.battlefield-design.co.uk)

Text © Alexander Querengässer 2019
Black and white illustrations © as individually credited
Colour artwork by Sergey Shamenkov © Helion & Company 2019
Maps drawn by George Anderson © Helion & Company 2019

ISBN 978-1-912866-60-1

British Library Cataloguing-in-Publication Data.
A catalogue record for this book is available from the British Library.

For details of other military history titles published by Helion & Company Limited contact the above address, or visit our website: http://www.helion.co.uk.

We always welcome receiving book proposals from prospective authors.

Contents

List of Illustrations & Maps

Illustrations

Graphs

Maps

Preface

The idea for this book came, after I was asked by Helion to write a book about the Saxon Army in the Great Northern War, which was the topic of my PhD. However, after having published two books about this topic – unfortunately for the English reader both are in German – I was looking for new challenges, even if I feel that I could do it even better in a third run, which I might tackle in a couple of years. I decided instead to focus on the origins of the Saxon army under John George III, which apart from a few early 20th century short PhD works is a very understudied topic, especially since military history has changed considerably since this time, asks new questions and forwards new theses, which have to be discussed.

I benefited greatly by discussing some central ideas of this book at conferences and at the universities in Dresden and Potsdam. I also owe many thanks to Martin Schröder, Oliver Heyn, Karin Tetteris, Katja Hartmann und Ulrich Herr, who helped me with material. Charles Singleton of Helion & Company proved himself to be an industrious and helpful editor, putting much effort into the research of images. Richard O´Sullivan read parts of the original script, making the work for my Helion editor Serena Jones easier – at least I hope so. Of course I am responsible for all mistakes that remain within the text.

Introduction

German military history in the early modern period used to be brushed over or simply reduced to a study of Prussian military history, but in recent years more and more studies have been published about other important but previously ignored armies of the Holy Roman Empire.[1] Although not entirely overlooked, even the Saxon military suffers from a huge gap between the Thirty Years' War, covered by Roland Sennewald's epic work,[2] and the Silesian Wars, which took place in the middle of the eighteenth century and are covered by the works of Stefan Kroll and Marcus von Salisch.[3]

This gap, broadly speaking between the Treaty of Westphalia and the Seven Years' war, is still something of a blank spot. Apart from a smaller work about the Saxon army at the famous camp at Zeithain in 1730,[4] the time of the Great Northern War is now covered by two works of this author.[5] Still awaiting study is the origin of the standing Saxon army during the period of the reign of Elector John George III. This is somewhat surprising, because the reign differed from earlier and later ones in that it was blessed with military successes. It represented a pause in the decline of the Electorate, from what at the beginning of the seventeenth century had been the most powerful princedom in the Empire after the Habsburg hereditary lands, to a second-

---

1 A good example for the last one is: Oliver Heyn, *Das Militär des Fürstentums Sachsen-Hildburghausen 1680–1806* (Veröffentlichungen der Historischen Kommission für Thüringen, Kleine Reihe 47) (Köln – Weimar – Wien: Böhlau Verlag 2015).

2 Roland Sennewald, *Das kursächsische Heer im Dreißigjährigen Krieg* (Berlin: Zeughaus Verlag 2013); Roland Sennewald, *Die kursächsischen Feldzeichen im Dreißigjährigen Krieg* (Berlin: Zeughaus Verlag 2013).

3 Stefan Kroll, *Soldaten im 18. Jahrhundert zwischen Friedensalltag und Kriegserfahrung. Lebenswelten und Kultur in der kursächsischen Armee 1728–1796* (Krieg in der Geschichte 26) (Paderborn e.a: Ferdinand Schoeningh 2006); Marcus von Salisch, *Treue Deserteure. Das kursächsische Militär und der Siebenjährige Krieg* (Militärgeschichtliche Studien 41) (München: Oldenburg 2009).

4 Reinhold Müller/Wolfgang Friedrich, *Die Armee Augusts des Starken. Das sächsische Heer von 1730 bis 1733* (East-Berlin: Militärverlag der Deutschen Demokratischen Republik 1984).

5 A brief overview is provided through: Alexander Querengässer, *Die Armee Augusts des Starken im Nordischen Krieg 1700–1721* (Heere und Waffen 21) (Berlin: Zeughaus Verlag 2013). However, this book is only based on the literature published so far. Far more detailed and based on archival research is my dissertation: Alexander Querengässer, Das *kursächsische Militär im Großen Nordischen Krieg 1700 – 1717* (Krieg in der Geschichte 107) (Paderborn e.a.: Ferdinand Schoeningh 2019).

rate power, by European and even Imperial standards, at the beginning of the French Revolution. The Saxon electors were generally more famous for their Maecenaship, buildings and art collections, than for being the kind of 'soldier-kings' produced by Brandenburg-Prussia (the Great Elector, his grandson Frederick William I, and most notably Frederick II). John George III is the exception to this rule. He reigned from 1680 to 1691 and earned himself the lyrical nickname of 'The Saxon Mars'.

While Saxony hired mercenary forces from time to time during and after the Thirty Years' War and even during the Franco-Dutch War 1672–1678, it was John George III who put these forces on a permanent footing. The transition from temporarily to permanent mercenary forces created new challenges, because the maintenance of troops created more work and called for more administrators. This does not necessarily mean that the state had to improve its administration in general, as is postulated by Michael Roberts,[6] because an effective military administration could be created within the existing framework of a state. However, the cost of a standing army absorbed a huge part of annual budgets, anywhere from a third up to 90 percent, as was the case in Russia. So the effects and repercussions of John George III's wish to create a permanent Saxon army and its effects on the relationship between the military and the state will need to be discussed early in this book. The question of how to finance the forces would involve critical negotiations between the Elector and his estates. The following chapters deal with organisational matters, how the army was recruited, what the social composition of the officer corps was, how the administration of the troops worked, how infantry, cavalry and artillery were organised and drilled and how they were expected to fight, where they obtained their uniforms, weapons and equipment, how discipline was maintained and what relations were like between the civil and military authorities. While these are all aspects of a 'modern' military history, focussing on a structural analysis, the last part of the book will tell the classical operational history of the campaigns in which Saxon troops fought between 1680 and 1691. A really complete modern military history cannot ignore campaigns, because these are the situations armies were created for, especially in this period. Good structures are no guarantee of success. Throughout history, huge and well provided armies have been defeated while small ragged bodies of troops have been able to win astonishing victories. The vicissitudes of war, the unforeseeable and maybe surprising influence of individuals have to be looked at and this can only be done by a description and analysis of campaign. 'The acid test of an army is war', said Alfred Vagts.[7]

No modern study of the Saxon army can ignore the solid foundation laid by Oskar Schuster and Friedrich Wilhelm Francke with their three volume work *Die Geschichte der Sächsischen Armee von der Errichtung bis in die*

6   Michael Roberts, 'The Military Revolution, 1560–1660', in: Essays *in Swedish History* (Minneapolis: Weidenfeld & Nicolson 1967), pp. 195–225.

7   Quot.: Alfred Vagts, *A History of Militarism. Civilian and Military* (London: Hollies 1959), p. 16.

neueste Zeit.[8] Covering nearly 300 years of Saxon military history it still is astonishing to a modern scholar how well researched the volumes are and how many interesting details they provide. However, typical for its time, the work concentrates on assembling facts, not in analysing them.

The same could be said about the dissertation of Walther Thenius, *Die Anfänge des stehenden Heerwesens in Kursachsen unter Johann Georg III und Johann Georg IV*.[9] This work is by nature able to provide even more relevant information than Schuster and Francke's general history. Decades before the 'war and society' approach became an established concept, Thenius followed the same path, maybe influenced by the theories of Hans Dehlbrück, but his work was printed in small numbers and is hard to find today. However modern his approach, Thenius' work is a child of its time, the nationalist pre-World War I era, which leads him to some anachronistic remarks, for example when describing the wish of the officers for a 'powerful Germanism' (*kraftvolles Deutschtum*).[10]

Some campaign studies are even older, for example Friedrich von Beust's *Feldzüger der kursächsischen Armee* from 1801.[11] Very detailed is the work of Paul Hessel and Carl Friedrich Count Vitzhthum von Eckstädt about the 1683 campaign which will be used here instead of the various modern works about the battle of Vienna, which are mostly based on this book.[12]

Some information can also be obtained from two extensive general histories of the early modern period. Gerhard Papkes' work for the handbook on German military history is a well-structured if in some parts outdated work which still provides an overview about army administration and finance.[13] English readers will find Peter H. Wilson's *German Armies. War and German Politics, 1648–1806* of equal value.[14]

---

8   Oskar Schuster/Friedrich August Francke, *Geschichte der Sächsischen Armee von der Errichtung bis in die neueste Zeit. Bd. 1* (Leipzig: Duncker & Humbolt 1885).

9   Walter Thenius, *Die Anfänge des stehenden Heerwesens in Kursachsen unter Johann Georg III. und Johann Georg IV.* (Leipzig: Quelle & Meier 1912).

10   Thenius, *Die Anfänge des stehenden Heerwesens*, p. 58.

11   Friedrich Constantin Graf von Beust, *Feldzüge der kursächsischen Armee, Bd.* 2 (Hamburg: Wilhelm Rößler 1803).

12   Paul Hassel/Carl Friedrich Graf Vitzthum von Eckstädt, *Zur Geschichte des Türkenkrieges im Jahre 1683. Die Beteiligung der kursächsischen Truppen an demselben* (Dresden: Wilhelm Baensch Verlagshandlung 1883).

13   Gerhard Papke, *Von der Miliz zum stehenden Heer. Wehrwesen im Absolutismus* (Handbuch zur deutschen Militärgeschichte 1648–1939 1) (Munich: Bernard & Graefe 1979).

14   Peter H. Wilson, *German Armies. War and German Politics, 1648–1806* (London: UCL Press 1998).

1 Saxony.

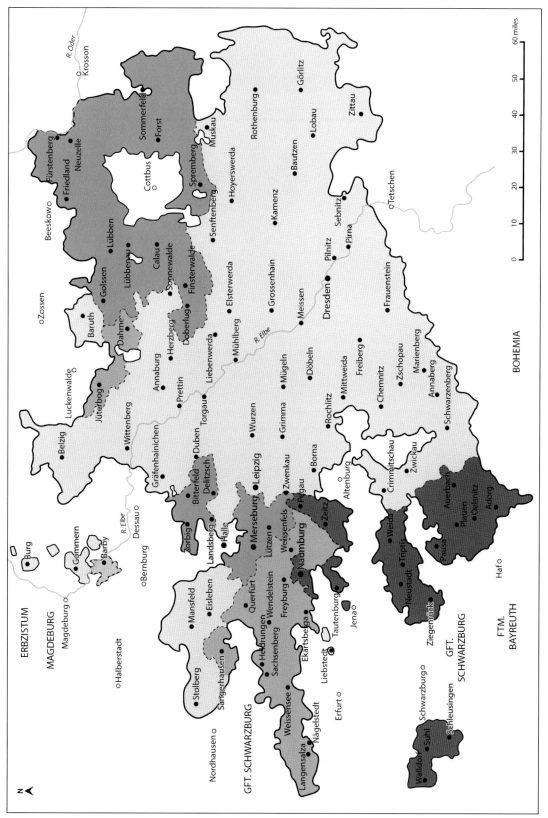

2 Strategic map of Central and Eastern Europe.

1

The Origins of the Saxon Army: From the Thirty Years' War to the Reign of John George II

Like many other German territories in the early seventeenth century electoral Saxony was trying to increase its military potential. Besides west European states, such as Spain, the Netherlands or to a lesser extent, France, even the wealthiest princedom of the Holy Roman Empire – second only to the hereditary lands of the Habsburg dynasty – could not afford to maintain permanent mercenary formations, except for small garrisons such as that for the capital Dresden, established in 1587.[1] Because of this, the Saxon elector like many other princes in the empire, tried to employ the services of his own population. In 1609 Christian II drew up a plan for the extension of the country's defences (*Landesdefensionssystem*), which he presented to the assembly of his estates in Leipzig in spring 1610, but the estates, always fearing the costs of permanent forces and the power they (might) give to their lord, rejected it.[2] He tried again, issuing a *Defensions-Ordnung* on 22 April 1611, but had to retract it in the face of widespread protest.[3]

The Elector died in June, and in November Hans von Gersdorf presented his successor, John George I, with a detailed outline for a defence system, complete with sketches of tactical formations to be employed by the troops. At a further assembly of the estates in Torgau in 1612 the Elector presented them with a third system, drawn up by the fortress colonel of Dresden, Centurio Pflug, and Colonels Karl von Goldstein and Jan von Schlieben. This final draft was accepted by the estates and became valid from 1 January 1613.[4]

---

1   August von Minckwitz, 'Die Besatzung zu Dresden von der mittelalterlichen bis in die neuere Zeit', in: NASG 7 (1886), pp. 235–277, here pp. 241–242.
2   Ernst Freiherr von Friesen, 'Das "Defensionswesen" im Kurfürstenthume Sachsen', *Archiv für die Sächsische Geschichte* 1 (1863), pp. 194–228, here pp. 195–196. More generally: Gustav Dietzel, 'Zur Militärverfassung Kur-Sachsens im 17. u. 18. Jahrhundert', *Archiv für die Sächsische Geschichte* 2 (1864), pp. 421–455.
3   Friesen, 'Das "Defensionswesen"', p. 196.
4   *Ibid.*, p. 196.

1 Elector John George I. (Engraving by Anselm von Hulle)

In the years following two regiments of foot with eight big companies each (520 men per company) and two regiments of chivalric horse (*Ritterpferde*) of 902.5 and 690.25 men were established.[5] The cavalry was provided by the nobility depending on the income of their manors, the infantry by the cities and districts depending on their population. The uneven number of horse already suggests that service in the field was being avoided by making a financial contribution. Additionally the system provided for 1,500 trench workers and 406 army wagons with two teamsters and four horses each.[6]

The militia character of this system can clearly be seen in its defensive use, because the soldiers provided this way could only be required in the defence of the electorate (even if it was not explicitly mentioned in the regulations). In many cases it represents more a kind of modernisation or at least regularisation of the old medieval feudal levy system, because the allocation of the chivalric horse – as the name suggests – is based on the vassal status of the nobility, while that of the communal infantry and the army wagons on the compulsory service of the cities and districts.[7]

The new militia system proved not very reliable during the Thirty Years' War and was quickly reduced to little more than a backup for an army built up with mercenary forces. In many cases people were unwilling to follow the call to arms. However, the army which invaded Lusatia in 1618 was supported by 240 army wagons, 926 trench workers, three companies from each regiment of foot and four companies of the regiment of horse (the originally two had just recently been reduced to a single one). The Saxon commander Count Mansfeld was less than impressed with them. In a letter to the Elector, he wrote: 'At home and on their own dung I will let them pass, but here I cannot entrust a post to them and will risk my reputation and honour with them.'[8]

For the hard fighting expected at the start of the war, Saxony, like other states, hired mercenaries. Under the command of Count Wolfgang von Mansfeld 12,000 men were raised and invaded upper and lower Lusatia. Bautzen was taken by siege and the rebel forces of the Bohemian estates driven out of Silesia. By 1624 nearly all Saxon regiments had been disbanded.[9] The Electorate enjoyed comparably peaceful years until Ferdinand II put

---

5   These calculations were based on the population. The quarter and half men were probably posed with money.
6   *Ibid.*, p. 197.
7   For the late medieval structure of Saxon armed forces see Alexander Querengässer, 'Kriegswesen und Herrschaftsbildung der Wettiner im späten Mittelalter', in *NASG* 88 (2017), S. 55–82.
8   Quot.: Friesen, 'Das "Defensionswesen"', p. 209.
9   See the very detailed study Sennewald, *Das kursächsische Heer im Dreißigjährigen Krieg*, pp. 17–42.

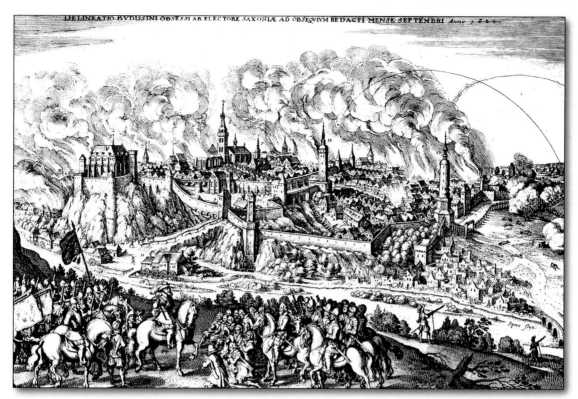

DELINEATIO BVDISSINI OBSESSI AB ELECTORE SAXONIÆ AD OBSEQVIVM REDACTI MENSE SEPTEMBRI Anno 1620.

2 In 1619 the siege of Bautzen in Lusatia (then a part of the Kingdom of Bohemia) was one of the first successful operations of the Saxon army in the Thirty Years' War. (Engraved by Matthäus Merian, 1593–1650))

the noses of loyal Protestant princes such as John George I out of joint with the *Reichsrestitutionsedikt*. When Gustavus Adolphus landed in northern Germany and Imperial and Liga troops crossed the border into Saxony, the Elector felt forced to join the Swedish and started to raise new troops.[10]

The question of service abroad, especially for the noble chivalric horse, remained a matter of contention. At a diet at Torgau in 1622, the nobility declared that their units would not operate outside Saxony. When in 1631 Saxony became a field of war, the two militia regiments of foot were used to garrison more than 20 cities and fortresses.[11]

The performance of the army, especially the militia units at the Battle of Breitenfeld in 1631, was poor, although not as bad as was claimed later by Swedish propaganda. The Saxon Army did not flee the battlefield after exchanging just a few shots with Tilly's troops, but only gave way after two hours of intense fighting during which it won vital time for Gustavus Adolphus' troops to finish their deployment.[12]

After the battle, the army was reorganised and invaded Bohemia. Some militia formations, including chivalric horse, took part in this operation.[13]

---

10   *Ibid.*, pp. 43–54.
11   Friesen, 'Das "Defensionswesen"', pp. 210–211.
12   Once more: Sennewald, *Das kursächsische Heer im Dreißigjährigen Krieg*, pp. 53–86. See also his essay: Roland Sennewald, 'Die Schlacht bei Breitenfeld am 7./17. September 1631', in: Maik Reichel (ed.), *Pappenheim. Daran erkenn' ich meine Pappenheimer. Des Reiches Erbmarschall und General* (Wettin-Löbejün: Verlag Janos Stekovics 2014), pp. 79–89.
13   Friesen, 'Das "Defensionswesen"', pp. 215–216.

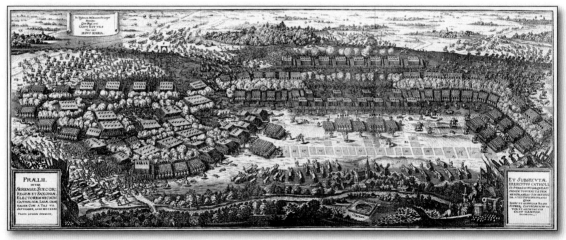

3 This Merian engraving shows the Battle of Breitenfeld. The Saxon army on the upper right flees from the battlefield. In reality, the Saxons held out quite a long time against the Imperialists, before the Swedes formed for battle. (Engraved by Matthäus Merian, 1593–1650))

The size of the army increased dramatically, reaching a peak of some 34,000 in 1635, making it second only to that of the Emperor. This army focused mainly on the conquest of Silesia where it inflicted a crushing defeat on an Imperial army at Liegnitz in 1634, but was itself defeated in 1636 at Wittstock – now on the Emperor's side again – and at the Second Battle of Breitenfeld in 1642. This last defeat led to a Swedish invasion which finally forced the Elector to beg for a ceasefire, which led to the armistice of Kötzschenbroda in 1645 and the Peace of Eilenburg in the following spring, in effect ending the Thiry Years' War as far as the exhausted Electorate was concerned. While the Peace of Westphalia guaranteed the Elector the *jure de armi et pacis*, the Saxon Army was nearly completely disbanded by 1651. Only a cavalry company of 121 men, a guard regiment of foot with 1,452 men and 143 artillery personnel remained in John George I's service.[14]

It would be wrong to say that Saxony had no armed forces in the years following, but these cannot be compared with the regular standing forces of states such as France, Spain, Austria or Brandenburg. The few permanent Saxon formations were guard formations, fulfilling a ceremonial task at court rather than a military one in the field. John George II, who reigned 1656–1680, was a flamboyant man with a love for the exotic. In 1660, he raised a company of Croats to serve in the Guard Regiment simply because he had fallen in love with their exotic dress.[15] For the same reason he raised a Swiss Palace Guard. Modern studies have so far neglected the fact that baroque princes seem to have collected exoteric guard units in the same way that they collected *objets d'art*. John George's grandson Frederick August I shared this passion with him, but his son John George III did not.

However, the Saxon army of these years cannot be reduced to fancy guard formations. In 1650 the estates asked for the complete disbandment of the militia system, but the discussions about this came to nothing. At another diet in 1653 a reorganisation of the system was discussed, based

---

14   Sennewald, *Das kursächsische Heer im Dreißigjährigen Krieg*, pp. 86–512.
15   For this formation see: Holger Schuckelt, 'Die Kroatenleibgarde zu Ross des Kurfürsten Johann Georg II. von Sachsen', in: Dresdner Kunstblätter 5 (2005), pp. 320–329.

on a memorandum by the experienced General von Schwalbach. All parties recognised the need for change; the Elector and professional military because they had seen how ineffective it was, the estates because they wanted to avoid useless costs. The proposal asked for two regiments of horse and three of foot formed of professional soldiers and paid with the help of the taxes raised from the noble manors and the cities instead of through their actual service. This progressive idea came to nothing, because the estates only wanted a disbandment of the militia system to save money, not the exchange of one system for another. In case of war they said, they were willing to pay for 4,000 mercenaries. John George I, on the basis of this offer, asked that the 4,000 men be kept on a permanent footing. This again was rejected by the estates so finally the old system was kept alive without significant changes.[16]

In 1661, John George II once more discussed a reorganisation of the militia with the diet. Initially all proposals were rejected by the estates, but two years later he was able to come to an agreement with them and published a new *Defensions-Recess*. The structure of the chivalric horse, army wagons and trench workers was not touched. But the new regulations changed the organisation of the regiments of foot, demonstrating the importance of infantry formations. The cities and departments of the Electorate now had to provide just 3,000 men in six companies (*Fähnel*) of 500 men each. Dresden, Wittenberg, Torgau, Leipzig, Zwickau and Freiberg were assigned as assembly areas for the companies. The captains who were commissioned by the Elector received a permanent payment (*Wartegeld*) taken from the tax revenue as did the *prima plana* and the 500 common soldiers provided by the cities and districts. The Elector guaranteed that he would not use these companies abroad and would call for them only in cases of emergency. The contingents of the individual communities were to assemble to drill four times a year, the companies three times a year, but not longer than two days. The muskets and bandoliers were provided by the Elector, swords, uniforms and shoes

John Georg von Arnhaimb Churfl Sächs General

4 Hans Georg von Arnim-Boitzenburg is here shown as a Saxon general. He had previously served under Wallenstein, and in 1631, and again after the defeat at Breitenfeld became an important organiser of the Saxon army during the Thirty Years' War. (Unknown artist)

5 This is a highly enlarged detail of an engraving showing a parade in Dresden. The figure represents Janko Peranski, lieutenant-colonel of the Croat Guard. The description of the engraving describes him wearing a leopard skin. (From Gabriel Tzschimmer, *Die Durchlauchtigste Zusammenkunft*, 1680)

16   Friesen, 'Das "Defensionswesen"', pp. 219–220.

6 John George II unsuccessfully tried to reform the Saxon army. (Artist: Johann Fink)

by the communities. In 1665 the six companies were assembled together for the first time but made a poor impression.[17]

The new system seems to have kept the deficiencies of the old one while causing more costs because of the payment of the officers. In 1666 John George II suggested to his estates, that 1,800 men of the new system should be disbanded while the other 1,200, still organised in six companies, should be kept on a permanent footing. Another 600 men should be used to increase the Lifeguards – the first attempt in Saxony to use the militia as a pool of recruits for the regular forces. Both suggestions were turned down by the estates, so in 1667 John George II disbanded the new system completely.[18] When Saxony had to send troops for the Imperial wars against the French, the country once more has to rely on hired mercenaries. In 1673 John George II raised several regiments of foot and horse.

In the meantime, some of the bigger principalities of the Empire had established *miles perpetuus* and used them successfully in several wars. Austria never disbanded all of its troops after the treaty of Westphalia, but kept the core of its formidable army and used it in the wars against the Ottomans in 1663/64 and the Dutch used it in their war against the French. Fredrick William of Brandenburg-Prussia, the Grand Elector had wanted to establish a standing army since he came to power and finally suceeded in 1653, using it in the Northern War (1655–1660) and the Scanian War (1674–1679). Brunswick-Lüneburg raised troops in the wake of a succession crisis in 1665 and did not disband them afterwards, but kept and used them against the Free City of Bremen. In 1671 the Welfen princes united their forces against the city of Brunswick which was taken by siege using 20,000 men and 100 heavy guns. The principality was subsequently regarded as one of the best-armed estates in the Empire, after Austria and Brandenburg-Prussia. Also one of the church-states of the Empire, the Prince-Bishopric of Münster, kept an army of at least 10,000 men under the command of Bernhard von Galen.[19]

In all of these states the *miles perpetuus* was not established just as an end in itself. As in previous times, armed forces were raised to be used for the benefit of the country or the dynasty. Austria tried to expand its territory into the Balkans and at the same time keep the French claims small. The Hohenzollern wanted to win sovereignty over the Duchy of Prussia, which later became the basis of the Prussian crown, even if it is foolish to draw a

---

17   *Ibid.*, pp. 221–223.
18   *Ibid.*, p. 223.
19   Jutta Nowosadtko, *Stehendes Heer im Ständestaat. Das Zusammenleben von Militär- und Zivilbevölkerung im Fürstbistum Münster 1650 – 1803* (Paderborn e.o.: Ferdinand Schöningh 2010).

straight line from the Northern War to the coronation of the Grand Elector's son in 1700. At the same time, Brandenburg still claimed Western Pomerania, which it believed should have come to it when the House of Griffin died out in 1637, but which was instead given to Sweden by the Treaty of Westphalia. Finally the Welfen were still pursuing their old desire to establish control over the bigger communities in north-western Germany.

Contrary to these examples, Saxony had no real territorial interests near to its border. It already controlled the important cities of the region and dominated the few tiny principalities bordering the Empire. The Electorate was a clearly defined entity. It bordered Brandenburg to the north and Habsburg territories to the east and south. War against these states was out of question, because both were strong and part of the Empire. It is often claimed that the complex institution of the Empire protected even the smallest principality. However, as can be seen by the examples of Bremen, Brunswick and Magdeburg, which had to take a Prussian garrison in 1666, with a mixture of military force and skillful diplomacy at the diet in Regensburg, the big fishes were still able to swallow the small ones. But for Saxony there have been no such morsels within its reach. To enforce claims on territories far away proved impossible, as could be seen by the example of the Jülich-Kleve succession crises in 1609 and the succession in Saxe-Lauenburg in 1689. In both cases Saxony staked out claims, but could not enforce them. The last possibility for a bigger expansion, would have been the annexation of the Prince-Archbishopric of Magdeburg (where August, the second son of elector John George I was administrator) but it was blocked in 1680, when August died and Brandenburg occupied the archbishopric according to the terms of Westphalia. According to them, Magdeburg in the case of the death of August was Berlin's compensation for Western Pomerania. Apart from these pragmatic reasons, which clearly argued against the establishment of permanent troops in the Saxon case, the size and performance of standing troops became an important yardstick for the reputation of a baroque prince.

After the treaty of Nijmegen was signed in 1680, the Saxon troops were reduced for the last time. Both the Lifeguards and the departmental regiment *Prinz Christian* were reduced to a few companies.[20]

---

20   Thenius, *Die Anfänge des stehenden Heerwesens*, p. 71.

2

The Army and the State

2.1 The Elector and His Estates

The compact nature of electoral Saxony in the seventeenth century disguises the fact that it was not one state, but a collection of very different territories. The only connecting tie was the ruling dynasty of the Wettins. The picture of the herald announcing his ruler's endless list of titles seems amusing to the modern spectator, but it is not an expression of vanity on behalf of medieval and early modern princes, it is an expression of the constitutional reality of their territories. John George III's full title was: 'Duke of Saxony, Jülich, Cleve and Berg, the Holy Roman Empires Arch-Marshall and elector, landgrave of Thuringia, Margrave of Meißen, Upper and Lower Lusatia, burgrave of Magdeburg, princely count of Henneberg, count of the Mark, Ravensberg and Barby, baron of Ravenstein, etc.' Some of these titles simply described offices, for example 'Arch-Marshall' was a medieval relic. The task was for centuries given to a family of the lower nobility, the Pappenheims, which titled themselves 'Hereditary Marshall'. The title 'Elector', too, simply gave the holder the privilege of electing the emperor and was bound to the Duchy of Saxony (Saxe-Wittenberg, in fact). Some titles, such as Duke of Jülich, Cleve and Berg, which was given to the Wettins during the first succession crisis in 1610, were simply claims to places held by others. However, these titles were not just an expression of wishful thinking; if another succession crisis were to blow up, a new claim could be presented. In an age, where warfare was often the result of succession crises, this made sense. Some territorial titles were relics, too, like that of Burgrave of Magdeburg, which came to the Wettins in 1423, along with the electorate. This, in theory, gave the family some judicial rights within the city, but, after the archbishopric and the city fell under the control of Prussia in 1680, there was no possibility of exercising them. Most of these titles, Duke of Saxony, Landgrave of Thuringia, Margrave of Meißen Upper and Lower Lusatia or Princely Count of Henneberg describe properties actually held by the Wettins. This does not mean that the territory ruled by Saxon electors was not recognised by contemporaries as one 'Saxony'. But in fact it was no more 'Saxony' than the Iberian possessions of the Habsburg kings were 'Spain', the lands of the Bourbon kings were 'France' or the alpine possessions of the Habsurgs were 'Austria'. The creation of early modern states was a complex and by no means linear or progressive process. While dealing with matters of foreign policy on the European stage, rulers seem to be representing a single state, but when dealing with internal matters they had to be careful to respect a variety of constitutional organisations, traditions and systems. By focussing almost exclusively on political and military events, classical historians often missed this point. Modern historians, concentrating more on structures and the process of nation building have tended to shift the balance too much in the other direction.

The old core territory of the Wettins was the margravate of Meißen, extending from the Erzgebirge in the south to Leipzig. To these the Duchy of Saxony around Wittenberg was added in 1423. Bounded on this duchy was the privilege of an elector of the Holy Roman Emperor. The margravate and duchy were merged in the sixteenth century and organised in *Kreise* (literally circles, in fact departments). The Wettins were also anxious to gain control of the three regional bishoprics of Meißen, Naumburg-Zeitz and Merseburg. During the reformation all three were incorporated, but in different ways. While the Bishopric of Meißen was disbanded and integrated into the departmental structure of the hereditary lands, Merseburg and Naumburg continued as bishoprics controlled by the respective chapters. Another huge territorial gain was achieved at the Peace of Prague in 1635. Saxony gained both Upper and Lower Lusatia, both margravates had been fiefs of the crown of Bohemia. They kept their own constitution and while their delegates were always invited to the general estates, the regional estates had much more influence in the process of decision making and neither margravate was included in the departmental system.

The complex constitutional structure was further complicated by the will of Elector John George I, who died in 1656. It declared that three duchies should be given to his three younger sons: August, Christian and William. Maybe it was because John George himself was a second son, who had been lucky enough to profit from the early death of his older brother, that he wanted to see his younger offspring properly taken care of. The three 'secundogeniture' duchies, Saxe-Weißenfels (for August), Saxe-Merseburg (for Christian) and Saxe-Zeitz (for Moritz) were not really cut out of the Electorate. The Dukes enjoyed the right to control internal and economic policies, but foreign policy was still made in Dresden for the whole country. The Dukes also had no seats in the Imperial diet, and tried to compensate for their lack of real power by making their mark on the landscape. August in Weißenfels and Moritz in Zeitz built huge, impressive modern baroque residencies, while Christian modernised the bishopric castle in Merseburg. The erection of these palaces and the cost of art collections and big courts had to be borne by the secundogenitures, which in turn reduced the tax revenue available to Dresden. While Saxony under John George I had to pay for one court, under his successors it had to pay for four.

Although the creation of palaces and courts proved a pleasant distraction, the Dukes were always on the lookout to increase their independence from Dresden and to obtain seats in the Imperial diet. Decisions made by the elector for the whole country were often seen as tutelage in these semi-autonomous territories. The ambassadors and delegates sent by the Dukes

7 A medallion praising John George III as defender of the Holy Roman Empire in 1688. (Dutch, by Philipp Müler. Photo: Alf van Beem, creative commons license CC0 1.0, public domain)

to other courts, notably Vienna and Berlin, complained about that and so weakened the political situation of the Electorate as a whole. With disgust the electoral ambassador in Berlin had to report home in 1688, 'how displeasing it was to hear the cousins of Merseburg and Zeitz speaking of his electoral Serenity as *Caput familia*.'[1]

Because of this tense relationship, John George III had mixed success in integrating the junior branches of the family into his army. The only prince of the house of Saxe-Merseburg to take up soldiering, joined the army of the Duke of Brunswick. He fell in the battle of Fleurus in 1690. The House of Saxe-Zeitz was apparently too small to risk its sons in the service of John George. Duke Maurice, who died in 1681, left just two sons, Maurice William, who was his heir and Christian August, who entered the church. However, the Saxe-Weißenfels branch did participate. Duke Christian, the younger brother of the ruling duke joined the army and became a *Generalfeldmarschallleutnant*.[2] And finally, in 1691, Friedrich Heinrich of Saxe-Zeitz took command of a regiment of dragoons.[3]

As in other European states – notably England – the estates could control the military, because they enjoyed the right to grant a budget for troops or raise special taxes. For collecting 20,000 thalers annually to pay 200 men of the 'Unterguardia', the garrison of Dresden, the estates in 1610 allowed the elector to raise a so called soldier-tax from the cities in the Electorate. These kinds of taxes were always restricted to a defined period, they were never permanent. The soldier-tax was granted for five years and later extended. When it ran out again in 1626, a year when the estates did not meet, the reigning elector John George I was forced to suspend the tax temporarily and, because he was not able to find another way to pay the 'Unterguardia', the soldiers went unpaid for nine months.[4]

The influence of war and the military on early modern state-building is still intensively discussed. According to the original military revolution theory put forward by Michael Roberts, the Swedish war effort in the late sixteenth and especially the early seventeenth century and the requirements of a huge military machine forced the state to build up a more effective administrative system.[5] This theory has been applied to many other armies and states by historians in the last 70 years, but has been criticised by experts such as Jeremy Black in general or David Parrott and John Lynn in their respective studies of the French army in the seventeenth century.[6]

---

1   Quote after: Frank Göse, 'Von der "Juniorpartnerschaft" zur Gleichrangigkeit. Das brandenburgisch-sächsische Verhältnis im 16. und 17. Jahrhundert', in: Frank Göse a.o. (ed.): *Preußen und Sachsen. Szenen einer Nachbarschaft* (Dresden: Sandstein Verlag 2014), pp. 44–51, here p. 51.
2   Commission from the 8 September 1688 SächsHsta DD 11237-209, fol. 118.
3   Commission from the 15 May 1691 SächsHsta DD 11237-209, fol. 284–286.
4   Friesen, 'Das "Defensionswesen"', pp. 201–202.
5   Roberts, 'The Military Revolution'.
6   John A. Lynn, *Giant of the Grand Siècle. The French Army 1610–1715* (Cambridge: Cambridge University Press 1997); David Parrott, *Richelieu's Army. War, Government and Society in*

THE ARMY AND THE STATE

In the case of the early standing army of Saxony no such causal relationship can detected. The army was created by the wish of the Elector with the consent of his estates which restricted it size to about 10,000 men. This seems rather small not only compared with the early modern mass armies of France, but also to the approximately 30,000 men which the economically much weaker Brandenburg-Prussia was able to put in the field in times of war. But such mere comparisons of numbers tend to ignore the question how far a state was really able to maintain its troops. David Parrott in his study of the French army under Richelieu had pointed out, that the size of the French army after 1635 exceeded by far the capability of the French administrative system to pay and supply its soldiers.[7] The German historian René Hanke stated in an essay, that whenever an early modern state increased the effectiveness of its administration, this development was not used to improve the miserable supply and payment of its troops but simply to increase their number.[8]

By contrast, the small Saxon army was comparatively well provided for by the state. That it was never increased beyond a certain level has to do with the kind of war it had to fight. While it was nearly constantly on campaign during John George III's reign, none of these wars were fought primarily for the direct interest of the Electorate. The Saxon army was fighting Imperial Wars either against the Ottomans or the French or it was on hire to foreign states. Of course, by supporting the Emperor against his two strongest enemies John George hoped not just to win glory on the battlefield but also goodwill that might result in political or territorial gains. It was a somewhat naive hope, because nothing was ever put in writing.

Uninvolved in wars of territorial expansion, John George saw no need to increase the size of his army or, consequently, his electorate's tax burden. This distinguishes him from the Great Elector in Brandenburg, who raised a large army to fight against Sweden for control of western Pomerania.

It was not until Saxony followed its own interests in the Great Northern war (1700–1721) that the military nearly tripled in size. This caused many problems, because in the first years of the war the estates were not willing to grant more money.[9] They were solidly against this war which in their eyes would only strengthen the position of the new elector Augustus the Strong – John George III's second son – by enabling him to become King of Poland. To increase the effectiveness of his military administration, Augustus

---

France, 1624–1642 (New York: Cambridge University Press 2001). From the numerous works of Black see for the seventeenth century: Jeremy Black, *Beyond the Military Revolution. War in the Seventeenth-Century World* (London: Palgrave Macmillan 2011).

7   Parrott, *Richelieu's Army*, pp. 366–396.

8   René Hanke, 'Bürger und Soldaten. Erfahrungen rheinischer Gemeinden mit dem Militär 1618–1714', in: Andreas Rutz (ed.), *Krieg und Kriegserfahrung im Westen des Reiches 1568–1714* (Herrschaft und soziale Systeme in der Frühen Neuzeit 20) (Göttingen: V&R unipress 2016), pp. 141–158, here p. 157.

9   I have extensively published on this topic, see: Querengässer, *Die Armee Augusts des Starken im Nordischen*; Querengässer, *Das kursächsische Militär im Großen Nordischen Krieg*. As a short English abstract: Alexander Querengässer, 'The Saxon Army in the Great Northern War', in: Steve Kling (ed.), *Great Northern War Compendium. A Special Collection of Articles by International Authors on the Great Northern War. Volume 1.* (St. Louis: LLC dba THGC Publishing 2015), pp. 245–254.

established a secret cabinet (*Geheimes Kabinett*) in 1704/06, which bypassed the old council.[10] Many historians see this as an attempt to create absolutist rule, but that concept belongs to later times.[11] It was really just an attempt to increase administrative effectiveness. Nevertheless, dynastic war and the demands of the armed forces were at last having an influence on the state building process within Saxony, a process that John George III's more limited ambitions had held at bay.

2.2 Establishing the Army 1680–1682

As already noted, after the Peace of Nijmegen the two Saxon Life Guard regiments and the *Prinz Christian* Regiment had been reduced to a few companies.[12] This was the last virtually total demobilisation of Saxony's armed forces. In November 1680, soon after his accession to the throne, John George III decided to build up a standing army. The idea was not completely new, as demonstrated by the different plans for the reorganisation of the militia developed in the reign of his father. A few months before his death John George II prepared another memorandum to be presented to a meeting the estates that the autumn. This memorandum asked for a increase of the *état* of military administration, the garrisons and the artillery. Most important was the creation of a small standing force of 1,000 horse, 3,000 foot and some field artillery. By taking into account the objections the estates had made to his previous suggestions, the Elector hoped this modest and relatively inexpensive proposal might meet with approval.[13] To strengthen his hand further, he disbanded most of the expensive, fancy, but militarily useless guard formations – most of which he had paid for out of his own pocket.[14] His son completed the process when he came to power late in 1680, by disbanding the Croats too. On the other hand John George III also preserved the rump formations of the field units whose troops had been discharged after Nijmegen. However, because most of the country, including the palace at Dresden, was still in the grip of the plague to which his father had fallen victim, John George III was not able to do much more in 1680. The commanders of the fortresses received orders to strengthen their defences and prepare their garrisons,[15] but this was more or less a formality as little could be done without cash.

The estates failed to meet. Just a few delegates assembled in Meißen in November. They approved money for the repair of the fortresses and the so-

---

10 Johannes Dürichen, 'Geheimes Kabinett und Geheimer Rat unter der Regierung Augusts d. Starken in den Jahren 1704–1720. Ihre Verfassung und politische Bedeutung', in: *NASG* 51 (1930), pp. 68–134.

11 As was first convincingly demonstrated by Nicholas Henshall, *The Myth of Absolutism: Change & Continuity in Early Modern European Monarchy* (London: Routledge, 1992).

12 See SächsHsta DD 11237-10809/2 and SächsHsta DD 11237-10809/7.

13 Thenius, *Die Anfänge des stehenden Heerwesens*, p. 7; 71.

14 The Swiss Guards were reduced, but not fully disbanded, see SächsHsta DD 11237-10809/4.

15 See SächsHsta DD 11237-207, orders for Col. Von Klengel (Dresden), 28 Aug/7 Sept. 1680, Col. Tittel (Leipzig) 30 Aug/9 Sept 1680.

called Seventh Penny, which was collected to pay for the existing formations. The next full assembly was then scheduled for November 1681.[16]

But John George did not want to let the year 1681 pass without doing anything towards the creation of an army. To recruit and organise regiments, he took the Brandenburgian colonel Ulrich Count von Promnitz into his service.[17]

In January 1681 the Elector ordered the two Life Guard regiments of foot and the *Freifähndel* to be combined into a single Life Guard regiment under the command of Lieutenant-Colonel Hans Heinrich Escher. Originally the regiment had nine companies, but soon was raised to 12. A year later it was renamed the *Von der Goltz* Regiment, while the electoral prince created a new Life Guard regiment with eight companies.[18]

On 28 August 1681 *Feldmarschalleutnant* Joachim Rüdiger Freiherr (Baron) von der Goltz, of Danish origins, defected from Brandenburgian into Saxon service. He became *Generalfeldmarschall* and was charged with establishing an army corps.[19] Promnitz became *Generalwachtmeister*.[20]

In November 1681 John George III finally presented his plans to the assembly of his estates. The negotiations give an impressive example of the comparable strong constitutional position of the estates and the weak position of the Elector. Knowing about the still weak constitution of his country in the aftermath of the plague, he first argued, that his own domains (*Kammergüter*) and the *Landesverwilligung* (a form of tax) could not maintain armed forces alone. He demanded the establishment of magazines to which each hide (*Hufe*) should contribute a *Metze* (old German dry measure for corn) of grain and oats. This was vital to supply an army of four regiments of horse, one of dragoons – each of 1,000 men – and four regiments of infantry, each with 12 companies of 200 men. For this the estates had to grant 1,000,000 thalers per year. Additionally the militia had to be raised to defend the borders in case the army left the country. Because the already existing units lacked payment, the estates should also grant a penny- and ember day tax (*Pfennig- und Quatembersteuer*), to pay them off.[21]

Knowing of the project of their Elector, the estates prepared their own *gravamina* (grievances) which were presented to John George III on 22 November. They demanded an investigation about the management of the domains and the questions, why more debts had not been settled in the recent years. They strongly rejected the request to raise the militia, arguing that the men could be trained anyway, but keeping them under arms would extract 3,000 good taxpayers from their work. They also complained about excesses and lax discipline of the existing formations, especially regarding

---

16   Thenius, *Die Anfänge des stehenden Heerwesens*, p. 8.
17   Frank Bauer, 'Zur Organisation und Struktur der kursächsischen Armee an der Wende vom 17. zum 18. Jahrhundert', *Sächsische Heimatblätter* 5 (1983), pp. 224–225;, Schuster/Francke, *Geschichte der Sächsischen Armee*, p. 97.
18   HstA DD 11338/252 Die Leibgarde zu Fuß, ohne Bl.
19   SächsHsta DD 11237-209, fol. 20–25; SächsHstA Dresden 11237/98 General Feld Marschalls Charge, fol. 2, 5.
20   Commission from 26 October 1680, SächsHsta DD 11237-209, fol. 131–132.
21   Thenius, *Die Anfänge des stehenden Heerwesens*, pp. 8–9.

billeting. According to them, officers and commissaries quartered their men without consulting municipal clerks. The two universities Leipzig and Wittenberg in particular moaned about soldiers being quartered in their villages, so that they did not generate any income which would be needed to pay the professors. The cities – drawing the darkest picture of the general state of the country – finally complained about the fact that soldiers took additional work, depriving their citizens of income. The billeted soldiers also pressed money and foodstuffs illegally from their hosts and so reduced the tax income. Regarding the small size of the existing forces, the *gravamina* grossly overstated their case as a first step for negotiations between prince and estates, giving the assembly the feel of an Oriental bazaar. Consequently, the estates were only willing to grant the country and drink tax (the oldest and most important ones), the meat penny and the expenses for ambassadors, while at the same time they halved the million for the troops and insisted the Elector not raise more troops than he could maintain. Magazines and money for the repair of the fortresses were not granted.[22]

John George first negotiated about the militia, but could not win any ground. Next he declared, that he could not maintain an army with less than 800,000 thalers and the magazines. He also wanted to establish the excise, an indirect tax which other countries such as Brandenburg already introduced to cover the costs of their military. This was another awkward topic, because once established the excise could become a financial instrument out of control of the estates which only could affect direct taxation. Instead the Elector offered another tax of one groat of each brought from a mill and a stamp tax.[23]

As a result, on 15 February 1682, the estates finally approved the meal groat for two years, a half penny for the ambassadors, the excise and the stamp tax. In return John George reduced his demands for the militia to 700,000 thaler. This sum had to be negotiated again and again through the following assemblies but did not change until the early eighteenth century. Another quite sensible request of the estates to use the army as a police force against the increasing nuisance of brigands and beggars was refused by the Elector. Finally on 5 March 1682 the estates even granted the grain for the magazines.[24]

Thus, the Elector was finally able to raise four regiments of foot with 12 companies each and four regiments of horse with and additional dragoon regiment of six companies each. For his personal guard, he raised just one company of horse and one of foot with two others stationed at Wittenberg.[25]

With the question of funding settled, extensive recruitment started in the spring of 1682. Because of his age von der Goltz was forced to relinquish command of the army in November 1683. His successor, the former *Generalfeldmarschalleutnant* Haino Heinrich von Flemming, was appointed on 15 February 1684, but it was not until von der Goltz's death, that Flemming also received his full rank, on 8 September 1688. Like his predecessor,

---

22   *Ibid.*, p. 9.
23   *Ibid.*, p. 9.
24   *Ibid.*, pp. 9–10.
25   Vgl.: Schuster/Francke, *Geschichte der Sächsischen Armee*, p. 98.

Flemming emanated not from the Saxon but from Brandenburgian nobility and joined John George's army in 1682. In 1691 he resigned and returned to the service of Brandenburg.[26] The employment of high- ranking officers from the army of the Great Elector indicates that the influence of that army on the newly created Saxon forces was great.

Another important office was filled by the *Kammerdirektor* (director of the chamber) von Bose. He became director of the *Geheime Kriegsratskanzlei* (Secret War Council).[27]

By as early as May 1682, John George III could muster his new army. It consisted of four regiments of horse, one of dragoons and six of infantry. The regiments of horse were cuirassiers with helmet and cuirass, while the dragoons were still viewed as mounted infantry. Nevertheless, the organisation of all five mounted units was the same, consisting of six companies, while the infantry regiments were formed of eight, except for the Lifeguards of foot which had 12. In total, there were 7,157 infantrymen, of whom initially two-thirds were musketeers and the rest pikemen. The cavalry, including the company of Lifeguards amounted to 3,222 men. The field artillery was fixed at 24 guns – although there were many more available in reserve in the arsenal at Dresden – 64 wagons and 142 men.[28]

Compared with the standing armies of Austria or the economically weaker Brandenburg, which at this time had about 30,000 men under arms, the Saxon force of 10,500 men seemed small. However, John George III had succeeded in creating an armed imperial estate (*Armierter Reichsstand*) and in doing so had demonstrably restored the power and political influence of his electorate. The number of troops raised enabled him to meet the requirement of the general estates that he not recruit more troops than could be paid for. Interestingly, under John George's successors, especially Frederick August, the size of the army was increased until on the eve of the Great Northern War it numbered about 25,000 men, while the basic budget of 700,000 thalers never changed. Obviously, this was only achieved in the face of great difficulties and by tapping other sources.

Table 1 The Saxon Army, 1682[29]

Cavalry and dragoons	Infantry
Kavallerieregiment *Graf Promnitz*	Regiment zu Fuß *Herzog Christian von Sachsen-Weißenfels*
Leibregiment zu Roß	Leibregiment zu Fuß
Kavallerieregiment *von Löben*	Regiment zu Fuß *von der Goltz*
Kavallerieregiment *von der Goltz*	Regiment zu Fuß *von Löben*
Dragonerregiment	Regiment zu Fuß *Flemming*
	Regiment zu Fuß *von Kanne*

26   Vgl.: SächsHsta Dresden 11237/98 General Feld Marschalls Charge, Bl. 2, 21–28.
27   Vgl.: SächsHsta Dresden 11237/813 Besetzung der Präsidenten Stelle, Bl. 2.
28   Vgl.: Bauer, Organisation und Struktur, S. 225.
29   Vgl.: *Ibid.*, S. 225.

2.3 Financing the Army

The assembly of the estates 1681/82 granted the quartember and penny taxes for six years. However, the 700,000 thalers per annum that this amounted to was not enough to maintain the army.

While this sum was voted by the estates as representatives of the whole electorate, the heterogeneous nature of the governance of the country meant it was not always easy to get the money out of some of the provinces. The biggest troubles were caused by the three Albertin duchies. While the Elector argued he had a right to raise taxes for the army because of his *jus de belli et pacis*, which included the right to sign alliances, quarter soldiers, raise recruits and collect money for the maintenance of the army, the Dukes countered with the argument that they enjoyed sovereignty over their lands.

In the case of Saxe-Weißenfels, as we have already seen, John George III had won the upper hand by 1681. On 29 June, Johann Adolf signed an accord and granted money, provisions and quarters for troops. In 1684 another one was signed, obliging the Duke to pay 7,000 thalers per annum. However, in 1686 John George III felt obliged to remind his cousin about this, stating that he was 21,000 thalers in default. Johann Adolf argued that the 1684 record only covered two years and that he was willing to pay 14,000 thalers at the Easter fair in Leipzig, which in the end he did. In 1687 he sent another 7,000 which were used for the maintenance of the mounted Lifeguards (3,000) and the *Plotho* and *Haugwitz* regiments (3,000 and 1,000 men respectively). Johann Adolf continually complained about the burdens of quartering troops. Indeed, these burdens must have been high, because his territories were situated along the main roads leading from Saxony to the Rhine, so troops taking this direction had to pass his major towns. In 1688, agents of the Elector and the Duke agreed in Leipzig to remit 2,000 thalers of that year's contribution to the budget along with 2,500 of the money in arrears to compensate for the exceptional burdens being borne by Saxe-Weißenfels. But only 2,000 were assigned to the regiment of Duke Christian, of which three-quarters were paid in cash. In 1689 John George demanded the full amount of 7,500 thalers and threatened to quarter a regiment of horse in the Duke's lands in case of refusal. His councillors Haugwitz and Bose had to remind him, that he had agreed to accept 5,000 each year, the rest being remitted because of continuing burdens from quartering. John George countered with the argument, that the Duke had other debts too, which were not related to his contribution for the army. In the years following this was fixed at 7,000 thalers which were rarely paid in full. Johann Adolf started to ignore the Elector in the negotiations, sending his complaints about his impoverishment directly to the Emperor, demonstrating once more how the creation of separate lands for the junior branches of the family weakened the electorate as a whole.[30]

Saxe-Merseburg constituted mainly of the old bishopric of Merseburg and Lower Lusatia. The dukedom was still administered through the diocesan

---

30 Thenius, *Die Anfänge des stehenden Heerwesens*, pp. 18–19.

chapter in Merseburg. There exist no records about the early negotiations between Dresden and the chapter, but in 1688 the Saxon councillors reported to John George, that Merseburg had paid an average 7,705 thalers over the preceding eight years.[31] Interestingly the difficulties of collecting taxes were much lower in Lower Lusatia, which was officially a part of the duchy. The *Kriegszahlamt* in 1692 presented a detailed list of the taxes collected over the last 10 years:

Table 2 Taxes granted and paid by Lower Lusatia, 1682–1692[32]

Year	Granted by the estates (in thaler)	Received
1682	23,334	11,956, the rest was used by the Regiment *Goltz*, but not reported to the war chest
1683	15,153	9,450, the rest taken by the Battalion *von Pflug* with receipt from Lt. Col. Trützschler, but not reported to the war chest
1684	15,646	15,633
1685	20,862	20,844
1686	22,600	8,521
1687 & 1688	38,214	24,954 & 14,865
1689	18,057	18,988
1690	10,057	19,557
1691	18,057	10,951 6 groschen
Total	189,980	172,800 thalers 6 groschen
Difference		−17,180 thalers 6 groschen

The reason for the difference in the willingness of the two halves of the duchy to make payments can be found in their localities and structure. Lower Lusatia was far away from Merseburg, in fact closer to Dresden, and surrounded by electoral lands. The estates had their own traditions which were much older than those of the secundogeniture. The table shows that the receipts from Lower Lusatia were generally very good, with notable exceptions in 1686 and 1691, while in 1682 and 1683 a part of the money seems to have been offset against other forms of contribution and in 1689 and most obviously 1690 even more money was paid, maybe to settle arrears of the years before. Most of this money was handed to the regiments quartered in Lower Lusatia, especially *Goltz*, *Flemming* and the Lifeguards.[33]

The situation was similar in Saxe-Zeitz, the 'successor' to the former bishopric Naumburg-Zeitz. On 3 July 1683 the contribution of the duchy was fixed at 7,000 thalers per annum, but only in 1682 and 1683 did the Duke make sizeable contributions. In the following years they were negligible. In 1688, the treasury presented a statement showing that just 27,416 thalers

---

31   *Ibid.*, p. 19.
32   Thenius, *Die Anfänge des stehenden Heerwesens*, p. 24.
33   *Ibid.*, p. 24.

6 groschen had been remitted in the past years and that 21,483 thalers 18 groschen were still outstanding.[34]

The *Kriegszahlamt* became so accustomed to this failure to make payments that for their own calculations they reduced the annual contribution of the duchies by 22,000 thaler.[35]

Unlike Lower Lusatia, Upper Lusatia was still part of John George's own territories. While the margravate sent its own delegates to the assemblies of the electoral estates it also had its own regional assembly. The latter was the more important of the two, because the decisions made there were binding and formed the instructions given to the delegates sent to the general assembly. From time to time, the general assembly made decisions not compatible with those of the regional parliament, but in such cases it was quite difficult for Dresden to enforce its will. However, the regional estates were generally cooperative. On 8 March 1682 they granted 50,000 thalers and a month later an additional 10,000 over two years (30,000 each year). In 1683 a further 18,000 were granted for the war with the Ottomans and on 30 May 1684 45,000. This makes for an average of not quite 31,000 thalers per annum in the years 1681 to 1685. About 30,000 were contributed each year until 1690, when it was decided to pay 40,000 per annum for the next three years.[36]

Very quickly the Elector began looking for additional sources of money. One was offered to him through the Imperial War constitution. The Empire was divided into 10 circles (administrative areas). The Saxon elector was head of the Upper Saxon Circle (*Obersächsischer Kreis*), which contained – beside Brandenburg-Prussia – many small principalities, for example the Ernestin dukes of Saxony and the Ascanian princes of Anhalt. While the small estates were not officially allowed to exchange the provision of troops to the bigger armed estates for subsidies, it was common practice. So Saxony could unofficially provide its troops on behalf of the circle and then collect money from the small princes in compensation.[37]

Because it was clear from the beginning that Saxon troops would fight either for the Empire or the Emperor (not necessarily the same thing), John George was looking for foreign help. Already in November 1682 Leopold I was trying to negotiate with the Elector about troops to be used against a potential Ottoman threat. These negotiations took time, because at the same time John George was looking to the Dutch Republic as paymaster for subsidies. A contract with the Emperor was signed not before 7 June 1683 – when a huge Ottoman army was already on the march to Vienna. Leopold I now officially granted John George the right to collect money from the small estates of the Upper Saxon Circle that could or would not contribute their own soldiers. Interestingly, the contract did not officially speak of defence against the Turks, but the French.[38] The reason for this lay in the fact that Hungary, where most campaigns against the Sultan's armies were fought, was

---

34   *Ibid.*, p. 19.
35   *Ibid.*, p. 20.
36   *Ibid.*, p. 25.
37   *Ibid.*, pp. 10–11.
38   *Ibid.*, p. 11.

not part of the Empire, unlike the territories threatened by the Sun King. A war in Hungary could be seen as a private affair of the Emperor, for which he had no right to demand help from the Empire. In 1691 the Emperor granted John George a further 300,000 thalers of subsidies, to be paid by the Upper Saxon and Franconian circles and the city of Frankfurt.[39]

Following the permission from the Emperor, Saxony started to sign several contracts with smaller principalities. On 10 January 1683, the princes of Schwarzburg agreed to pay 22,000 thalers in return for exemption from billeting, beginning on the following 1 February. Apart from 2,500 thalers which went to the contingent of Saxe-Weimar, 19,500 was to go directly to the Elector's army. This sum was to be paid in monthly instalments for the next three years unless peace was declared in the meantime. In the event of the money not being paid, the Elector kindly offered to send in his army to help collect it! The contract was extended in 1686 for another two years. Now the princes wanted to pay 20,000 thaler. Because it could not be avoided, that Saxon troops were quartered in Schwarzburg territories on their march to the Rhine, the cost of this was deducted from the monthly payments. Once more the contract was extended in 1688. Obviously the quartering of troops was a pressing burden on the small countries, because their negotiators constantly demanded that their contributions be lowered in compensation. Regrettably, after the Nine Years' War with France broke out, the number of billeted troops increased, and from 3 May 1689 the subsidies were raised to 33,000 thalers for just nine months. The princes paid most of this sum but were permitted to retain 3,612 thalers as compensation for the burdens of billeting. For 1690 the Emperor instructed the princes to pay another 40,000.[40]

A similar agreement was negotiated with the Barony of Schönburg, a small principality belonging to the Emperor in eastern Vogtland. The barons (*Herren*) agreed to pay 3,866 thalers 16 groschen each year, but just for the war against the Ottomans. However, in some years they failed to pay the full amount, so in 1687 the *Zinzendorf* Regiment was quartered in their territories. In October 1688 the contract was extended and in July the next year von Bose, on the Secret War Council, reported to the elector that he had received 9,600 thalers from the barons.

The counts of Reuß fell in with the Imperial request on October 1683 and promised 8,720 thalers for that year and 9,280 for the next, to be paid quarterly. While the first instalments were paid on time, increasing burdens for quartering Saxon troops on their march to the Rhine caused trouble here too and in January 1686 the counts begged to have two instalments remitted because quartering so far had generated costs of 40,000 thaler, but John George stuck to his guns. He even increased the burden by billeting three companies of the *Zinzendorf* Regiment in Reuß territories. The year after, the counts once more begged to be relieved from quartering, because otherwise they would not be able to pay the 145 *Römermonate* assigned to them. Now the Elector argued that the three companies could not cause much extra cost, because they were only given quarter and service. On the contrary, through

---

39   SächsHsta DD 11237-10822/11, without fol.
40   Thenius, *Die Anfänge des stehenden Heerwesens*, pp. 11–13.

spending their money in the Reuß territories, they would even increase the counts' income. In the same year they wanted to let the agreement run out and wait for another Imperial request. However, John George argued in 1688 that he was still providing troops for the Empire, so Reuß should pay. Giving way to this pressure, the counts granted 8,320 thalers for another year. With the official declaration of war on France through the Empire in 1689 this sum was nearly doubled. In May 1689 they were obliged to pay 15,000 for nine months, part of which was used for the *Grenadiercompagnie Reuß*. In 1690 the annual contribution was raised one more time, to 19,200 thaler, a sum which had to be paid each year until 1694.[41]

The abbey of Quedlinburg – the only Imperial estate ruled by a woman – offered 4,000 thalers per annum in 1684 but paid only occasionally. In April 1685 the Saxon war chest had to state, that no money for 1684 was paid and the first contribution for 1685 was also missing. At the beginning of 1686 another 3,000 thalers were paid. In April, Abbess Anna Dorothea of Saxe-Weimar wrote to John George that she could only raise a further 1,300 and that with the greatest difficulties and wanted to cancel the accord of 1683. Again the Elector sent troops – an easy matter, because Saxony was protector of Quedlinburg. In 1687 no money seems to have been paid, maybe the cost of quartering covered the contribution. In 1688 the abbey paid three of its four contributions which in the year after were raised to an annual total of 7,680 thalers and the year after that to 10,533 thaler. Because receipts are registered in Saxon books, it is possible that these sums were offset against the cost of the quartering of troops.[42]

The counts of Stollberg were ordered by the Emperor in 1683 to pay 130 *Römermonate* per month, but, surprisingly, upon the assembly of the Circle in 1684 a figure of 145 was offered with a ceiling of 4,000 thaler. However, by 19 December only 2,000 thalers had actually been collected and by 1685 the counts were 10,000 thalers in arrears and tried to excuse the deficit in terms of the costs of quartering the troops passing through their lands. This seems a little unlikely, because most of their territories were in the Harz Mountains. In 1685 Saxony reduced its requirement to 3,500 thalers per annum but also demanded quarters for a company of infantry. Despite this, by 1687 the city of Wernigerode owed the Saxon army 3,000 thaler. The city council argued that Wernigerode was a vassal of Brandenburg and paid its dues to Berlin. As the place was occupied by Brandenburgian troops, it even ignored repeated orders from the Emperor to pay the money to Saxony. This conflict also demonstrates how the two electorates struggled for influence over all the small estates in middle Germany. Instead of attempting to bring the Hohenzollern to heel, Leopold I simply placed a further demand, for 5,600 thaler, at the door of the counts in 1689. He cut this sum to 4,700 the next year, but clearly getting money from the Harz was no easy matter, because according to the books of the *Kriegszahlamt* the counts owed it 9,534 thalers in 1691. The councillors of the counts then presented another petition to reduce the amount owing to 4,675, remit the money from Wernigerode and to take into

---

41   *Ibid.*, pp. 13–14.
42   *Ibid.*, pp. 14–15.

account the costs of quartering Saxon troops. Surprisingly Councillor von Bose accepted this, maybe because he knew that not much more could be had. Nearly matching the 4,700 thalers ordered by the Emperor, this money seems to have been paid quite regularly over the next few years.[43]

The counts of Mansfeld, who ruled an area rich in silver mines in late medieval times, came more and more under electoral Saxon control from the sixteenth century onwards. In 1683 Leopold prompted the counts to pay 4,000 thalers for that year and 7,000 for the following. However, subjected to sequestration because of high debts, they were not able to pay their allocations for 1683 and 1684. The first money reached the Saxon war chest in 1685, so that in 1686 5,000 thalers could be forwarded to the regiment *Reuß* and in 1687 another 7,750 to the regiment *Kuffer*. A new record signed in 1686 obliged the counts to pay 7,000 thalers in each of the next two years. However by 25 September 1688 they were 13,439 thalers in arrears. In the same year the counts were imposed upon for a further 7,000 thaler, which was not paid until 1689. Many towns of the county were willing to pay their share, however Eisleben begged to be excused as it had recently suffered from a huge fire. It was relieved from these payments and from other taxes for five years. Because of the war with France the subsidies for the county as a whole were raised to 10,676 thalers a year but they had to be collected by force, because many communities were reluctant to pay.[44]

The county of Barby originated from a junior branch of the dukes of Saxe-Weißenfels and consisted of a territory not part of the electorate. Its Count Heinrich wrote a lengthy letter to his electoral cousin in 1683 describing in flowery, baroque language the miserable state of his small principality, which was financially exhausted because of quartering and had been devastated by the flooding of the Elbe and the collapse of a dam. Because of this he could see no possibility how the small town of Barby and his five wretched villages could raise 1,800 thalers a year. Certainly, the high water of the Elbe had wrecked Saxon territory too, so John George III accepted the excuse and the matter of subsidies was not raised again before 1689. On 30 April of that year the elector informed Heinrich that, because of the war with France, the contribution for Barby was fixed for a half company or 294¾ Thalers a year. If the count had trouble collecting this money, he would lend him soldiers for this task. Again Barby begged for remission but in the next year the contribution was raised to 500 thalers per annum. This sum was paid in 1690 but in the summer of 1691 Heinrich wrote to von Bose that he was able to collect 500 thalers but needed 600 to repair the Elbe dams. This time Dresden threatened armed intervention, but to no avail. In 1692, when Barby's debts amounted to 1,000 thaler, the count stated blandly that the money had been stolen from the town hall.[45]

The two baronies of Blankenhain and Kranichfeld belonged to the family von Gleichen. Dresden in October 1684 demanded 800 florins each year dated back to 1 January 1683. However in December this amount was

---

43   *Ibid.*, pp. 15–16.
44   *Ibid.*, pp. 16–17.
45   *Ibid.*, pp. 17–18.

lowered to 500 and the quota for 1683 remitted. But the barons showed themselves unwilling to pay and in 1689 John George III restored their contribution to 800 florins and billeted a company of horse on them. In 1690 the von Gleichens begged for remission and also in the year following they paid nothing.[46]

Notwithstanding all the difficulties of collecting money, all the excuses and complaints which were typical for the time and troubled even the Great Powers, the contributions of the small estates of the Circle were important, maybe even vital for the maintenance of the Saxon army. They are also evidence of Saxony's increasing role as a regional power. This fact is of great interest not just for the history of the Saxon army, but for the Empire as a whole. While it was always argued that the Empire as an organisation protected the small and tiny estates from being pocketed by the bigger ones, the latter process was ongoing and in the end proved irreversible. Resistance to the taxes and subsidies levied on the smaller territories gave John George III the right to collect the money by offsetting the amount due against the cost of quartering of troops on the recalcitrant areas, which had the added benefit of lowering the burden on the taxpayers of the electorate proper. All in all, the small territories granted an annual total of 50,000 to 60,000 thalers or 7.1 to 8.5 percent of the budget granted by the Saxon estates.

It was always a problem for the early modern state, to find a working balance between a budget granted, real cash collected, and costs. While the administration always worked on the basis of the former and the latter, the huge discrepancy between the granted contributions of the provinces and the taxes paid caused many difficulties, because the bills for uniforms, food or the payment of the men could not be negotiated or discussed. Thus in 1682, even though the estates had granted 700,000 thalers for the army and its costs were estimated at 660,332, the *Kriegszahlamt* only received 591,458 thalers in tax and in the end an additional 79,547 had to be granted, to make up the actual amount required.[47] In December, Colonel von Kanne was informed that the war chest was empty and there was no money to pay the rations for his men. Because his regiment received additional money for hiring recruits, the War Council decided that the captains of the individual companies should pay back the deductions for clothing to the men, so that rations could be paid.[48] Nobody asked the Colonel or the captains if this money was already spent, so it is quite probable that the officers had to pay for the food themselves.

Back in September, *Oberkriegszahlmeister* von Lämmel had reported that by the end of the year expenditure would have outstripped income by 183,000 thaler. The differences which opened up so often between monies granted, taxes collected, cash distributed to the war chest and hard coin available for the troops were also a result of the fact that there was no central tax chest, but several, and the money for the army – and other requirements of state – was pieced together from various sources, including the electoral

---

46   *Ibid.*, p. 22.
47   *Ibid.*, p. 25.
48   SächsHsta DD 11237-884, without fol., letter from the War Council to Col. Kanne of 1 December 1682.

chest. The latter contribution was not included in the 700,000 granted by the estates. This administrative chaos – by no means exclusive to Saxony – was further increased by corruption. The aforementioned *Oberkriegszahlmeister* Lämmel was convicted of this crime after his death. Rumours about his venality existed throughout his career, but because 'putting one's hand into the honey pot' (to use a phrase of the Prussian King Frederick II) was considered normal at the time, neither John George III nor his successors took the matter too seriously. Only after Lämmel's death was it discovered that he had stolen an astonishing 300,000 thaler. One reason that he had got away with it for so long was because he had succeeded in presenting himself as saviour, always finding new resources to tax or creditors to borrow from.

Table 3. *Kriegszahlamt* tax receipts 1681–1688[49]

1681	
Quartember tax	91,030 thaler
Zuschuß	76,196 thaler
Total	167,226 thaler
1682	
Pfennig- and Quartember tax	498,889 thaler
Vorschuß	49,752 thaler
Mahlgroschen	41,567
Stamp tax	1,250 thaler
Total	591,458 thaler
1683	
Pfennig- and Quartember tax	582,173 thaler
Mahlgroschen	40,595 thaler
Stamp tax	4,700 thaler
Total	627,468 thaler
1684	
Pfennig- and Quartember tax	656,418 thaler
Mahlgroschen	700 thaler
Contribution from the knights	8,470 thaler
Total	665,588 thaler
1685	
Pfennig- and Quartember tax	586,983 thaler
Contribution from the knights	29,780 thaler
Total	616,718 thaler
1686	
Pfennig- and Quartember tax	671,177 thaler
Vorschuß for quarters of garrison officers	6,822 thaler
Total	677,999 thaler
1687	
Pfennig- and Quartember tax	669,812 thaler
Contribution from the knights	1,257 thaler

---

49   SächsHsta DD 10024-9123/2, fol. 1.

Vorschuß for the quarters of the garrison officers	8,187 thaler
Total	679,256 thaler
1688	
Pfennig- and Quartember tax	680,338 thaler
Grand Total	**4,706,051 thaler**

Table 3 shows a deduction presented by the *Kriegszahlamt* in 1689. According to this, it never received the full 700,000 thalers from the tax. However, the years from 1686 to 1689 fall short by less than 35,000 thalers (five percent). All in all it received 4,706,051 thalers in eight years. This seems less, but the early years of 1682 and especially 1681, when the army was being raised, affect this total amount.

While the official budget was spent on running expenses – pay, provisions, uniforms etc. – there were also substantial extraordinary costs. These consisted of the money for hiring new men, *Wartegelder* (for the time in which they have not been assigned to a certain unit or office), travelling expenses (*Verschickungsgelder*), costs for the acquisition or repair of muskets, guns and wagons and of course the repair of fortresses, for which no money was granted by the general estates. These outgoings may have exceeded 100,000 thalers each year. Documented are extraordinary expenses of 162,591 thalers in 1688,[50] a year when additional expenditures were required for manifold things, because the army had to be mobilised for the war with France.

While in general the estates were not unwilling to grant money for extraordinary costs, it was always interlinked with other demands. In 1685 John George presented the general estates with a claim for 114,275 thalers 3 groschen in addition to the 719,543 thalers 16 groschen for the subsistence of his troops. The western circles of Thuringia, Neustadt, Erzgebirge and Vogtland had to cover quartering costs of 91,379 thalers 11 groschen 8 and a half pennies and there were arrears of 51,730 thalers 6 groschen 4 pennies. The estates showed signs of willingness to grant these sums but asked that the recruiting for filling up the regiments sent to Venice should be discontinued for the rest of the year. John George accepted this on 24 July, but four days later the estates also wanted the 114,000 thalers to be dropped and even that the remaining troops be further reduced. The Elector's claims seem to be rather unreasonable, given that the troops sent to Venice were to be maintained by the Serenissima and the arrangement should have reduced the burden on the war chest. Maybe the estates had this in mind, because on 30 December they granted a generous 18 and a half pennies! The Vogtland and Neustadt circles received a tax reduction of 6 groschen for each infantryman (in the Thuringian and Vogtland circle 4 groschen 6 pennies) and 12 for a cavalryman (9 groschen in Thuringia).[51]

---

50   *Ibid.*, p. 26.
51   *Ibid.*, pp. 27–28.

In 1688 John George III demanded an additional 310,992 thalers for the mobilisation of the army. However, the *Obersteuerkollegium* protested and stretched the payment over three years. Furthermore 100,000 thalers should be granted as credit for the war chest in 1689 and 1690.[52]

These difficulties in raising taxes did not lead to immediate administrative reforms – and so once more the example of John George's army runs counter to the theory that early modern military developments had a direct influence on state-building processes. Instead, the government tended to engage in bureaucratic shortcuts. Rather than receiving money from the war chest, which in turn received it from the *Obersteuereinnahme*, many regiments had the taxes of certain circles assigned directly to them so that the war chest just received receipts.[53] This perhaps lessened administrative problems but makes it more difficult for the historian to get a reliable overview of the military budget. Also, the departments and provinces did not always send their proofs of expenditure to Dresden straight away, sometimes they kept them to offset the demands of electoral tax collectors. The records themselves were well kept, but the flexibility, or laxity, of the system makes it difficult to see what was claimed, what was granted, what was paid in direct taxes to Dresden and what in cash or other forms (billeting, etc.) to the regiments, and what may have got lost along the way.

52   *Ibid.*, p. 28.
53   *Ibid.*, pp. 26–27.

3

Administration

3.1. The Central Organ of Administration: The *Geheimes Kriegsratskollegium*

While Saxony had no standing army units before 1682, the war-torn years of the early seventeenth century – especially the period of the Thirty Years' War – forced the elector to establish administrative structures which survived every retrenchment and in fact became permanent. On 2 May 1634 the Secret War Chancellery (*Geheime Kriegskanzlei*) was officially created, directed by a high war commissar (*Oberkriegskommissar*) or general war commissar (*Generalkriegskommissar*), who was only hired for the period that hostilities lasted. His staff was small: a secretary and a second writer (*Kopist*) for copying all orders. The quartering and provisions system and the war chest were subordinated to the War Chancellery.[1]

However, the responsibilities of the War Chancellery were limited and the fact that only the secretary was retained in post during peacetime robbed it of all possibilities for military reforms or any kind of improvement. Many matters of organisation, the recruitment of troops and general financing were still in the hands of the Secret War Council which in turn lacked professional know-how. Up until then all administrative tasks such as quartering, supplying, paying, recruiting, assembling of units or whole armies, marches and so on were done by a general war commissar (*Generalkriegskomissar*) who also took care of the general war chest (*Generalkriegskasse*). This could barely be done by one man in time of peace let alone when Saxony needed to hire troops in times of war. After the armed forces had been brought onto a permanent footing it was recognised that it was too huge a task for a single person.[2]

The idea for a new administrative organisation can be credited to Christoph Dietrich von Bose who proposed it in November 1681. On 25 January 1682 he became the first director of the *Geheime Kriegskanzlei* which had not previously even existed on paper. While a decree announcing its formation was published on 4 March, the unexpectedly urgent mobilisation

---

1   *Ibid.*, p. 29.
2   Schuster/Francke, *Geschichte der Sächsischen Armee*, p. 111.

of the army for its first campaign in 1683 thwarted its proper instigation. After the return from Vienna a commission was created on 14 November to examine the shortcomings that had come to light in the army. The commission was composed of von Bose, High Court Marshall Friedrich Adolph von Haugwitz and *Feldmarschalllieutnant* von Flemming. In December they suggested the formation of a war council. This was approved by the Elector and, on 24 January 1684, a plan for a secret war chancellery was drawn up. The commission was in effect to be transformed into a permanent chancellery which had control over everything concerning the army such as payment, billeting and discipline. It would become the organisation through which the Elector controlled all branches of his army.[3] The Secret War Council (*Geheimes Kriegsratskollegium*) was officially established as a new administrative department for the army on 14 February 1684 and commissions were signed in the following weeks granting the councilors a monthly remuneration of between 200 and 250 thaler. It was expected that one of them would accompany the army on campaign. The composition of the council changed throughout the years and the number of members was not fixed. In 1689 there were just two until, on 20 May, a third was assigned in the person of the baron of Haxthausen.[4]

Subordinated to the new organisation was the Secret War Chancellery (*Geheime Kriegskanzlei*), consisting of a war councillor, a secret war secretary (*Geheimer Kriegssekretär*), another secretary (first *Kalkulator*, later *Sekretär*), a chancery clerk (*Kanzlist*) and a steward. While the Secret War Council had no established working rooms (because all its members had other official duties), the Secret War Chancellery was located in the third floor of the Taschenbergpalais, directly opposite the castle in Dresden. John George III bought the palace in 1684 for 6,000 thaler. The Secret War Council also held its meetings here, chaired by the war secretary. He also received the muster records and had to issue passes, recruiting patents and other official documents in which he was aided by the ordinary secretary and the clerk.[5]

Subordinated, too, was the General War Payment Bureau (*Generalkriegszahlamt*), consisting of the general war paymaster (*Generalkriegszahlmeister*), a secretary (*Kopist*) and a field kasserer (*Feld-* or *Kriegskassierer*)[6] with aids. The paymaster had to travel at each New Year, Easter and Michaelmas to Leipzig to receive the contributions of the estates of the Upper Saxon Circle. This underlines the importance of this fair city as a middle European centre of finances, because this money often was not paid in cash, but in money orders, secured or issued through merchants. The *kasserer* had to present the monthly accounts to the War Chancellery and the High Commissary.[7]

---

3   Thenius, *Die Anfänge des stehenden Heerwesens*, pp. 34–35.
4   Schuster/Francke, *Geschichte der Sächsischen Armee*, p. 111; Thenius, *Die Anfänge des stehenden Heerwesens*, p. 35.
5   Thenius, *Die Anfänge des stehenden Heerwesens*, pp. 35–36.
6   From 14 April 1686 Johann David Haußmann, SächsHsta DD 11237-211, fol. 4; from 23 April 1691 Johann Christian Döbner, *Ibid.*, fol. 8.
7   Thenius, *Die Anfänge des stehenden Heerwesens*, p. 36.

In 1680 Johann Lämmel became war paymaster,[8] a position he held for more than 20 years, being elevated to general war paymaster in 1686.[9] He became an important figure in providing money and especially credit for the army, much of which came from his own resources. But he seems to have lined his own pockets while doing so and after his death, as mentioned above, it was calculated that he might have purloined as much as 300,000 thaler. However, it is difficult to be certain because of the complex web of his finances. Of course, this web was created in the service of the Elector, who for example sent Lämmel to obtain money from the financial centres at Hamburg and Amsterdam,[10] but it was the man, not the system, that made the contacts with individual creditors. This again shows that the early modern state needed the private clientel networks of its officials, because the administrative organisation was in all too small for its tasks.

The commissariat general also had to follow the orders of the Secret War Council. At the beginning he was assisted by a ration officer (*Proviantverwalter*), an aide who had to supervise the supply depots (*Magazines*).[11]

Little information exists about the field postal service (*Feldpost*). The techniques of early modern (military) communication are a vital field for understanding how campaigns were managed and armies far from home administered. However, until recently this field was widely ignored by historians.[12] While we have some information that some kind of military postal service existed during the 1683 campaign, the next time we hear about it is in 1691, when John George III gave orders – the oldest of an Imperial prince – from the baths in Teplice to his army on the road to the Rhine through such a service. The Elector published a short, three page, instruction for the creation of the service, calling it a court and field postal office (*Hof- und Feldpostamt*). This might have been the result of struggles between the family Thurn and Taxis, who had the Imperial postal service monopoly, and the von Paars, who organised Lower Austrian and court mail. While Thurn and Taxis claimed to be the only party permitted to organise a postal service in the Empire, the von Paars argued that military affairs were part of the court mail and so fell within their competency. The ongoing debate resulted in serious delays in military correspondence, forcing John George to act.[13]

The new Saxon military postal service does not seem to have been a bespoke institution, simply being made up of members of the civilian postal service, who followed the army into the field and were given the title of field postal service. The system was managed by high postmaster Wilhelm Ludwig Daser with headquarters in Leipzig – which as a centre of finances and trade was of course also one of communication. He provided a postal

---

8   Commission from September 1680, SächsHsta DD 11237-211, fol. 1.
9   Commission from 3 April 1686; SächsHsta DD 11237-211, fol. 3.
10 Passport from 22 May 1684; SächsHsta DD 10024-13541/35, without fol.
11 Thenius, *Die Anfänge des stehenden Heerwesens*, p. 37.
12 Recently the overview: Kai Lohsträter: '"an einer minut ein großes gelegen". Militärische Kommunikation, Kriegsberichterstattung und Zeit vom 16. Bis zum 19. Jahrhundert', *Militär und Gesellschaft in der Frühen Neuzeit* 21 (2017), pp. 97–145.
13 *Ibid.*, pp. 107–110.

service between the army and Saxony twice a week, although this was not particularly difficult as the dispatches were simply inserted into the Imperial postal system for delivery! Because the postal service was seen as a kind of regal right, there were inevitable conflicts with other services when the army operated abroad. The Saxon field post arrangement caused immediate protests from the Austrian colonel-general postmaster (*Oberst-Generalpostmeister*) Count von Paar, the Thurn and Taxis family and even the Emperor himself. Von Paar hampered Saxon communications, because he felt his privileges threatened. However, because neither the Emperor nor the Reichstag, where other princes put forward similar proposals for the organisation of military postal services, could settle the matter, John George III was finally successful. He also signed a bilateral agreement with Thurn and Taxis which definitely helped his case, because the Imperial post organised by the family was still indispensable for communications. With this contract Thurn and Taxis also won a round in their private dispute with the von Paar family.[14]

The reach of the Secret War Council, which in theory was a central administrative organisation, was in practice limited by the complex constitution of the Electorate. Its authority was limited to the hereditary lands and the principality of Querfurt (which was a part of the secundogeniture Saxe-Weißenfels which did not belong to the Electorate). Both the Lusatias, the former bishoprics and the County of Henneberg were supervised by the Elector and the Secret Council. However administrative matters very often were also discussed in the war collegium first and results presented to the Secret Chancellery which issued orders accordingly. The interplay between the civilian and military personnel of these organisations probably aided the working of a structure which on paper was very complex.[15]

Thenius tends to underrate the efficiency of the new administration, arguing that it was not able to stop complaints about military excesses.[16] However, as we shall see later, these were typical teething problems of early modern armies. Levels of efficiency should be judged in terms of the reduction of complaints, not the failure to achieve their eradication, which was impossible.

3.2 Commissaries and Logistics

Commissaries were important arbitrators and organisers in the Early Modern Military. During the Thirty Years' War nearly every European army established a commissary system to organise marches and quartering. Both officers and civilian administrators could be hired for these duties. The latter were sought after, because they were familiar with regional and local facilities,

14 For the Postal Service see: Gustav Schäfer, *Geschichte des sächsischen Postwesens vom Ursprunge bis zum Uebergang in die Verwaltung des Norddeutschen Bundes* (Dresden: Verlag R. von Zahn 1979), pp. 95–96. The information given in this work is the same used by Thenius; Kai Lohsträter: "'an einer minut ein großes gelegen", pp. 110–111.
15 Thenius, *Die Anfänge des stehenden Heerwesens*, pp. 37–38.
16 *Ibid.*, p. 38.

for the former it was an attractive job because it offered a chance for extra income. This in turn could also open windows of opportunity for corruption. In Saxony there were many grievances about commissaries ignoring tax norms and tables when billeting troops and extorting seven thalers a month from their own hosts, because in the electorate at that time commissaries were unpaid.[17]

These troubles continued after the war and forced John George II in 1676 at the behest of the cities and landowners that only locals with good knowledge of the region should act as commissaries. During marches two nobles should guide the troops and report to the circle director (*Kreishauptmann*). A suggestion by the gentry that the circle directors themselves should act as guides was rejected by the Elector[18] with good reason, because very often regiments of a marching corps used more than one road or were quartered over a wide area, impossible for the busy directors to cover.

The year after, John George II appointed two commissaries each for the Vogtland and Thuringian circles and one for each for the others. These men not only had to organise the movement of Saxon troops, but also those of other regiments passing through the Electorate. However, they were instructed to do their utmost to prevent troops entering the electoral territories. If this was not possible, they should assign quarters and report the fact to Dresden. The commissaries also received a regular payment of six thalers now, reducing the need, if not the possibility, to extort money from citizens. Extraordinary costs for messengers or writers were paid separately.[19]

John George III further improved this system by appointing two commissars for each circle from 1683 onwards:

Table 4 Commissaries for the Saxon circles in 1683[20]

Circle	Commissars
Kurkreis	Hartmann Ludwig von Witzleben Count Burkhardt von Bodenhausen
Meißnischer Kreis	Georg Rudolf von Lüttichau Heinrich von Polenz zu Görzig
Leipziger Kreis	Christian Sigmund von Holzendorf Staz Friedrich von Fulle
Erzgebirgskreis	Caspar Sigmund von Berbisdorf Georg Christoph Römer
Thüringischer Kreis	Christoph Caspar von Goldacker Georg Rudolf von Hessler
Vogtländischer Kreis	Karl Bose zu Mylau Hans Georg von Schönfels

17 *Ibid.*, p. 29.
18 *Ibid.*, pp. 29–30.
19 *Ibid.*, p. 30.
20 Thenius, *Die Anfänge des stehenden Heerwesens*, p. 30.

The provinces belonging to the secundogenitures also had commissaries assigned. Merseburg, Zeitz, the two Lusatias and the Vogtland and Neustadt circles maintained their own, paid by their princes. Saxe-Weißenfels enjoined an exceptional position and got the commissaries assigned to their territories from Dresden.[21]

Payment increased remarkably, demonstrating the importance of the commissaries. Georg Rudolf von Lüttichau from the Meißen circle received an annual 500 Thalers from 1 September 1684 or more than nine times as much as a commissary under John George II.[22]

Their remit was restricted to the borders of their circles or provinces. However, under special circumstances the Elector could expand them, for example for the march of an army corps. The mandate of January 1682 clearly described their authority under point VIII: 'When it comes to marching the route of march will be designated by the Secret War Council with knowledge of the *Generalfeldmarschall* and sent to the war commissaries who will lead the troops and billet them, the officers in turn being ordered to follow them.'[23]

On 1 January 1688 the commissaries were subordinated to the *Geheime Kriegskanzlei*. This sent the marching orders and routes to them, so they could organise billeting. The officers of the regiments were advised to obtain the billeting letters in time.[24]

Mediating between the military and civilians and dealing with the secundogeniture dukes, made the job a hard one. Staz Friedrich von Fulle twice forwarded his resignation – on 10 November 1683 and 8 May 1686. He lived in a state of continuous conflict with Duke Christian of Saxe-Merseburg, who disliked him because of his vigorous handling of his duties.[25]

However, as soon as a commissary forwarded his resignation, the cities and landowners begged for a new one, underlining the importance of their work. Sometimes they recommended one of their own ranks, but the final right to appoint them was the Elector's.[26]

The increase in payment is indicative of the increasing amount of work. While under John George II commissaries only had to organise marches and billeting from time to time, in the time of the *miles perpetuus* most of their time was consumed creating a system of permanent billeting.[27] This and the increasing numbers of troop movements after the war with the Ottomans started in 1683 caused the commissaries to hire subordinates, because they could no longer supervise every marching regiment and every quartered company themselves. This in turn increased their expenditure, causing the estates to attempt to forbid the hiring of subordinates, which would have been a damaging measure had they succeeded.[28] Collaboration between

---

21 *Ibid.*, p. 31.
22 *Ibid.*, p. 31.
23 Quot.: Mandat über die Neuordnung des Militärwesens im Kurfürstentum Sachsen, January 1682.
24 Thenius, *Die Anfänge des stehenden Heerwesens*, p. 31.
25 *Ibid.*, p. 31.
26 *Ibid.*, p. 31.
27 *Ibid.*, p. 31.
28 *Ibid.*, pp. 31–32.

commissaries and officers did not always work smoothly. The marching regulations of 1691 complained, that 'on occasions officers dared to treat the commissaries with contempt; marching not according to their orders but following their own inclination and quartering themselves ...'[29]

The post of general or high war commissary was recreated in 1681.[30] It was not designed to be permanent, but in fact it was occupied until 1694 in succession by various officers – the personnel about every two years. In cases of troop movements the whole officer corps of the army was subordinated to him, giving the general war commissary an equal rank to that of the *Generalfeldmarschall*, at least within his restricted area of competence. He also supervised musterings, countersigning the muster roles confirming the companies were at full strength and that the captains had not hired disabled men, servants or even non-existant recruits. He was paid a monthly 125 thalers with perks, if he had to take the field.[31]

This was the case in the Nine Years' War. On 25 January 1689 Hans Ehrenfried von Klemm was named high war commissary. His instructions also charged him with the supervision of the war chest and the supply of provisions, for which he could hire subordinates. He distributed the regiments' monthly requirements of cash in return for receipts signed by the regimental quartermasters. The receipts would be accompanied by the monthly quartering bills of their units. During campaigns the organisation of a field hospital was also part of his duties. For all this work the general war commissary had a very small, not yet fixed staff. Normally this consisted of a deputy war commissary, a secretary, two scribes and a steward, but the occupation of these posts depended on the finance available. In 1691 with the appointment of Hans Adam von Schöning as *Generalfeldmarschall* the commissary business was directly subordinated to him.[32]

All commissaries had an officer's rank and pay. The *Generalkommissar* was similar to the *Generalwachtmeister/majorgeneral*. The highest commissary's income was initially on a par with that of the *Generalquartermaster* or the *Generalauditeur*. However, after the beginning of the Nine Years' War the payment of the *Generalquartermaster* suddenly nearly doubled from 120 thalers in 1689 to 200 in 1690, while that of the *Generalauditeur* remained at 105 thaler. The implication being that good organisers were in short supply after another great west European war erupted.[33]

The General War Payment Department (*Generalkriegszahlamt*), the field postal service (*Feldpostamt*) and the army's medical department were all under the control of the War Commissary. It also possessed its own provost under a *Kapitänleutnant de Guide* with the authority to enforce ordinances and arrest insubordinate or corrupt officers. While in theory the War Commissary itself was subordinated to the Secret War Council (until

---

29   Quot.: March-Reglement 1691.
30   Thenius writes 1682 (Thenius, *Die Anfänge des stehenden Heerwesens*, p. 32), but in SächsHsta DD 11237-213, without fol., there is a letter of Friedrich Rommel, who received his commission as high war commissar on 28 August 1681.
31   Thenius, *Die Anfänge des stehenden Heerwesens*, p. 32.
32   *Ibid.*, pp. 32–33.
33   *Ibid.*, pp. 44–45.

the appointment of Schöning) it retained a certain degree of independence, because the commissaries had the right to report directly to the Elector or the *Generalfeldmarschall*.[34] This perhaps explains why at the end of John George's reign this institution was directly subordinated to Schöning himself.

Within the borders of the Electorate the soldiers were provisioned from depots. The assembled estates refused to supply these depots in 1681, but they changed their mind in March 1682. The noble manors, which were generally exempt from paying taxes, were also exempted from this duty, as was the church. Five depots were established, in Dresden, Leipzig, Wittenberg, Zwickau and Langensalza. In 1683 the neighbouring villages were allowed to pay money rather than provide corn or oats. However, both corn and money came in irregularly so that in 1685 the *Geheimes Kriegsratskollegium* ordered a detailed registration of taxable property and formulated a penalty of 100 thalers for each *Hufe* of land (*Hufe* = a square measure, comparable in meaning to the English 'Morgan') which had failed to supply its quota. A list from 1685 shows a total of 3,545 bushels of corn on hand, contributed from 56,720 *Hufes*. These were stored as follows: 573 in Wittenberg, 1,107 in Dresden, 299 in Zwickau, 809 in Tennstädt and 757 in Leipzig.[35] Outside the Electorate it was not clear who had responsibility for providing for the troops. John George demanded rations from Imperial commissaries which in turn demanded that the Saxons supply themselves. This led to many situations in which the soldiers had to help themselves, which in turn led to a decree in 1686 forbidding them from doing so.[36]

The depots were originally under the *Chambercollegium*, but in 1683 came under control of the *Generalkriegskommisariat*. Their first administrator was Christoph Kaphahn who was also secretary for provisions.

The *Equipageamt* was responsible for the train for which a captain was commissioned in 1688. In 1683 each company received wagons with six horses, but in the next year the wagons were abolished and the companies just used packhorses.[37]

---

34   *Ibid.*, pp. 33–34.
35   SächsHsta DD 10024-9118/7, fol. 3..
36   Mandat 1686, § 3.
37   Thenius, *Die Anfänge des stehenden Heerwesens*, pp. 105–106.

4

The Officer Corps

While recruiting men for a new army was already a demanding task, getting experienced officers was even more difficult.[1] Under these circumstances it seems astonishing, that the majority the 267 officers within the army in 1682 were veterans. Ninety percent had served before and just a minority of them in foreign armies. One hundred and ninety-three officers (72 percent) had served in Saxon regiments before. This shows a certain continuity in the military tradition of the Electorate, and demonstrates that lack of a standing army does not mean a lack of considerable military forces, just a lack of continuity, which is demonstrated by the fact that 84 of these officers also served in foreign armies. Some officers went through seven different career stations, on average, the officers served two different princes before. About a fifth had served the elector of Brandenburg before, while a considerable number also served the Emperor and the Netherlands.

Service times varies between six months and 38 years for a Saxon and between one and 32 years for foreigners with an average service time respectively of 10 and 12 years.

4.1 The High Command: *Generalfeldmarschälle* Under John George III

When the Saxon army was mobilised in the Swedish period of the Thirty Years' War, it was placed under the command of a general field marshal (*Generalfeldmarschall*) and led by an officer of that rank until 1641. Not surprisingly, when John George III set up his standing army, he recreated the post and appointed the experienced Joachim Rüdiger von der Goltz, to fill it at a salary of 1,200 thalers per month. Von der Goltz had served in the Brandenburgian and Danish army before.[2]

---

1   As a modern study regarding the officer corps see Andreas Dethloff, *Das kursächsische Offizierskorps 1682–1806. Sozial-, Bildungs- und Karriereprofil einer militärischen Elite* (Hamburg: Verlag Dr. Kovac 2019), here pp. 273–274.
2   SächsHsta DD 11237-212, without fol; Schuster/Francke, *Geschichte der Sächsischen Armee*, p. 98; Thenius, *Die Anfänge des stehenden Heerwesens*, pp. 38–39.

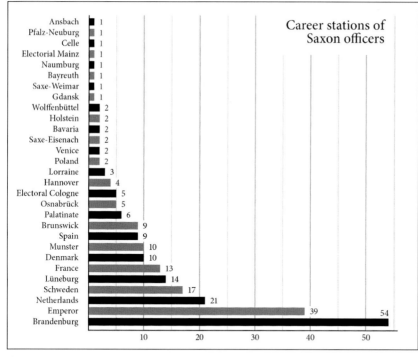

Career stations of Saxon officers

Location	Number
Ansbach	1
Pfalz-Neuburg	1
Celle	1
Electoral Mainz	1
Naumburg	1
Bayreuth	1
Saxe-Weimar	1
Gdansk	1
Wolffenbüttel	2
Holstein	2
Bavaria	2
Saxe-Eisenach	2
Venice	2
Poland	2
Lorraine	3
Hannover	4
Electoral Cologne	5
Osnabrück	5
Palatinate	6
Brunswick	9
Spain	9
Munster	10
Denmark	10
France	13
Lüneburg	14
Schweden	17
Netherlands	21
Emperor	39
Brandenburg	54

As Von der Goltz was a sick man and unable to take the field, it is likely that he was chosen principally for his organisational skills. In 1683 he was relieved from command.[3] Officially he kept his position until his death on 26 June 1688, but from 1683 onwards most of his duties were performed by his lieutenant Heino Heinrich von Flemming, who was also from the Brandenburg service. Flemming joined John George's army on 8 April 1682.[4] Two years later he became a member of the Secret War Council. His high payment of 2,000 thalers a month – more than von der Goltz received – is ample proof that his duties were greater than those normally performed by a *Feldmarschalllieutnant*. Only after von der Goltz's death, was he raised to the rank of *Generalfeldmarschall*, on 26 September 1688.[5]

His successor – Hans Adam von Schöning – was one of the most controversial figures of his age. During the siege of Bonn in 1689 he had a disagreement with his comrade General von Barfus which resulted in a swordfight (not a regular duel). As a consequence Schöning was relieved the year

8 Joachim Rüdiger von der Goltz was responsible for the organisation of the army, but was too old and sick to take the field any longer. (Engraver unknown)

---

3   SächsHsta DD 11237-209, fol. 37–38, letter from John George III. from 14 November 1683.
4   SächsHsta DD 11237-212, without fol.
5   Thenius, *Die Anfänge des stehenden Heerwesens*, p. 39.

9 Heino Heinrich von Flemming was Saxony's leading field officer and succeeded von der Goltz as field marshal in 1688. (Engraver unknown)

10 Hans Adam von Schöning was the last Feldmarschall under John George III and later influenced the reforms of his son Frederick August. (Engraving by August Christian Fleischmann))

after and went to Saxony, where John George III immediately made him *Feldmarschall*.[6]

Schöning profited from the fact that the new Elector of Brandenburg, Friedrich III, had recalled *Feldmarschall* Heino Heinrich von Flemming. This illustrates the problem of employing senior officers from other states. As Brandenburg-Prussia became more and more involved in the Nine Years' War, its elector needed every experienced officer he could lay his hands on and, as von Flemming's liege lord, he felt he had a right to demand his services. Needless to say, John George disagreed and wrote to Friedrich on 28 April 1690, saying '[how] sinister it would be to my army, if a general of such experience should be withdrawn from it.' He reminded Frederick that a decade earlier his [Frederick's] father, the Great Elector, had guaranteed, that Flemming would be allowed to stay in Saxon service. He also offered the opinion that the Brandenburg army was 'sufficiently provided with good generals, wheras I suffer from a lack of them.'[7] This last comment might be read as implying that the Saxon elector was not satisfied with the quality of his officer corps, but one has to be careful interpreting baroque complaints,

---

6   Commission from 9 April 1691, see SächsHsta DD 11237-209, fol. 90–93.
7   Quot.: Frank Göse, 'Ressentimentgeladenheit und Rezeptionsbereitschaft: Bemerkungen zum kursächsisch-preußischen Verhältnis auf dem Gebiet der Militärgeschichte von der Mitte des 17. bis zur Mitte des 18. Jahrhunderts', in Christian Th. Müller / Matthias Rogg (ed.), *Das ist Militärgeschichte! Probleme – Projekte – Perspektiven* (Paderborn o.a.: Verlag Ferdinand Schoeningh 2013), pp. 383–398, here p. 389.

because exaggeration was a very common rhetorical device and in this case may have been used to add weight to his argument in favour of being allowed to keep Flemming. Despite John George's protestations the Pomeranian left the army, but fortunately Schöning proved to be more than his equal. He received a monthly payment of 1,800 thalers plus an additional 200 for his service as a member of the Secret War Council.[8]

The *Generalfeldmarschall* was the Elector's lieutenant acting on behalf of the ruler from whom his authority stemmed. The diary Flemming kept from 1687 gives a detailed insight into his job. He received the regimental reports, officers' petitions for leave, promotion or retirement, and reports about judicial matters (excesses, desertions and other crimes).[9]

4.2 From Lieutenant to General

Beneath the *Generalfeldmarschall* were the *Feldmarschalllieutnants*, whose numbers were not restricted. They led the army in the absence of the Elector or the *Generalfeldmarschall*, but their authority was not as great. The *Feldmarschalllieutnant* always had to ask the elector or *Feldmarschall* for approval of his orders, or – if that was not possible – had to call for a council of war with his officers. They were each paid 500 thalers a month and commanded their own regiment of foot with the rank of colonel (which generated additional remuneration).[10]

The commanding officers were assisted by a general staff. This however cannot be compared with the permanent administrative and planning organisation that carries that name today. Normally, some, or all, of the general officers taking part in a campaign were considered part of the staff and were invited to the war council as the important *gremium* (committee) for operational and tactical decision making. Beneath this there was a network of administrative aids consisting of commissaries, the Quartermaster General and Auditor General with their respective lieutenants, a court secretary, the paymaster and the members of the Secret War Chancellery. Normally, a secretary, a registrar, four copyists and a steward were also considered part of the staff but did not take part in councils. In the field, surgeons, a staff quartermaster, a staff courier, a guide, a general wagon master, and two field couriers could be added to this list.[11] Although the assemblage has the appearance of being somewhat haphazard, a provision report for the 1682 campaign indicates that on that occasion at least, the number of senior administrative officers was fixed.[12]

During John George's reign, the Saxon army had no such rank as a general. This was introduced under his son, replacing that of *Feldmarschalllieutnant*. Later, in the 1680s, came lieutenant leneral (*Generalleutnant*), followed by

---

8   Thenius, *Die Anfänge des stehenden Heerwesens*, pp. 39–40.
9   *Ibid.*, p. 40.
10 *Ibid.*, pp. 40–41.
11 *Ibid.*, pp. 41.
12 *Ibid.*, pp. 41.

the *Generalwachtmeister*. The latter rank was redesignated as major general towards the end of the decade. Senior colonels commanding temporary brigades made up of two or three regiments were entitled to be referred to as brigadiers, but it was not an official rank.[13]

Regiments were run and very often maintained by their colonels. While an official rank in most cases, colonel was more an honorary title, as regiments were raised and owned by officers of higher rank and in reality managed by the lieutenant-colonels (*Oberstleutnant*). The *Oberstwachtmeister*, later major (from about 1689), was responsible for drilling the regiment and was the third man in hierarchy. All three had their own companies and so a position and additional income as captains. However, the rank of major seemed to have not existed in all regiments. The first officer presented with this title was Georg Rudolf von Schönfeld of the *Kurprinz* infantry regiment in September 1689, but the rank is not mentioned in the *Marschreglement* of 28 March 1691.[14] The major, or *Oberstwachtmeister*, had to prepare the weekly reports for the colonel and was responsible for the preparation of courts-martial. For this he was assisted by an adjutant, who acted as a kind of secretary and deliverer of orders.[15]

At the company level, there were three different officer ranks. The captain was head and commander of the company and very often also financially responsible for it. This gave him considerable power, which the Elector gradually tried to undermine. The captain's assistant was the lieutenant, of which there was just one per company at this time. He kept the company journal and was responsible for the weapons. The oldest lieutenant in the regiment was called captain lieutenant and ranked immediately below the youngest of the regiment's captains.[16] The junior of the three company officers was the ensign. He inspected the troops and wrote reports, which had to be submitted to the major.

Not unimportant were numerous volunteers who joined the army in the hope of getting a permanent commission. Volunteers were sometimes nobles without formal military training, hoping to learn the job by doing it, or unemployed officers from other armies or units. In a dispatch sent by Flemming to the Elector in 1690 during the siege of Mainz, he recommended a lieutenant-colonel, three captains, four lieutenants and four ensigns, who were serving as volunteers and who deserved to be considered for positions should they become available.[17] Vacancies could sometimes occur on a large scale. When Saxony sent three regiments to Venice in 1685 the men were drawn from all the existing infantry regiments and the resulting vacancies were filled immediately. When the troops sent to Venice came back, 48 officers along with several hundred enlisted men had to be put on waiting pay, which amounted to 13,903 thalers 12 groschen alone in 1687.[18] Many of

---

13   *Ibid.*, p. 44.
14   *Ibid.*, p. 43
15   *Ibid.*, p. 57
16   *Ibid.*, p. 43.
17   *Ibid.*, p. 48.
18   *Ibid.*, p. 50.

the officers joined other regiments as volunteers when the Nine Years' War started in the following year.

If nobles joined the army as officers or if officers were promoted, they had to swear a new oath in the presence of an auditor or a general adjutant and a commissary.[19]

Soldiering constituted a central part of the ethos of many German princes. John George III tried to forbid his nobles from serving in foreign armies in 1681. However, the estates protested:

> Because the case is, that the nobility of this country, because it has no access and nearly no resources left to preceed and preserve [we back your Serenity], by the intended recruitment and placing of war offices on the natives, if they are qualified for them, at first to refrain, especially to take those of knighthood into his own services or at least allow them, that they follow the path of war outside the country and train theirselves in war in a foreign princes payment.[20]

So the Elector was not able to abolish military service abroad, as did the Prussian king Frederick William I early in the eighteenth century. The appeal of the estates demonstrates another problem. It seems that the majority of the Saxon nobility lacked the financial means to take service as colonels or captains in the Saxon army. This is in marked contrast with the situation in the army of Louis XIV, where, as John Lynn and David Parrott have shown, noble colonels and captains helped to preserve their respective units with their own capital and credit.[21] So when the Saxon estates complained that military service was an opportunity for many nobles to earn money, it reveals these men of title lacked the resources to help defer the cost of maintaining Johann George's army. A few examples suggesting this was nevertheless the case can be found in the sources. In 1685 Major (*Oberstwachtmeister*) Elias von Haußmann presented a bill to the War Council for 1,004 thaler, which he had spent out of his own pocket for his company and for which he needed to be compensated. The circumstances were examined carefully and it was decided, that Haußmann should indeed be reimbursed. Interestingly, the war chest contained a receipt for about half the amount, signed by the commander of the regiment, who had collected the money from the men's wages and then kept it for himself rather than passing it on to the major.

This system for maintaining companies was later criticised during the Age of Enlightenment and by the Prussian reformers. They saw it as stealing from the state, a view which has survived right into modern scholarship.[22]

---

19 See the record SächsHsta DD 11237-208, which is full of rescript of promotions, naming the persons present.

20 Quot.: Frank Göse, 'Der Blick über die Grenzen: Brandenburgische und sächsische Adlige im 16. und 17. Jahrhundert', *Sächsische Heimatblätter* 2 (1996), pp. 68–76, pp. 74.

21 Lynn, *Giant of the Grand Siècle*, p. 236: 'More than any other factor, the burdens imposed by the maintenance system dictated that officers be well-to-do. Throughout the seventeenth century, the king and his ministers recognized the imperative that colonels and captains possess the means to maintain their units.'; Parrott, *Richelieu's Army*, p. 320.

22 For example: John Childs, *Warfare in the Seventeenth Century* (London: Cassel & Co 2001), S. 100.

THE SAXON MARS AND HIS FORCE 1680–1691

But this view is based on the image of a modern state, which did not exist in the seventeenth century. Thenius pointed to the fact that some officers of low rank complained about slow advancement and had trouble covering their living costs with their low pay, while on the other hand young nobles of wealth could be captain at just 23 years.[23] This suggests that personal wealth of commanding officers was still considered important for the subsistence of the troops. Even though Saxony maintained an army more in line with its economic resources than other countries, especially the major powers, mobilising private fortunes for state interests was still part of the political system. The implication of this should be borne in mind. A captain taking over a company also took over its debt, a problem which prevented many capable men from receiving advancement.[24] In this light, early modern military units appear to be half state, half private institutions and the officers of this time half state employees, half private investors.

The selling of commissions was finally forbidden to Saxon colonels in 1687,[25] which shows that the Elector was trying to strengthen his grip on his officer corps.

In the same year, after listening to the proposals of the *Feldmarschallleutnant* and the other regimental commanders, John George III also ordered that officers could only be assigned when confirmed by him personally. This step seemed necessary because he was not satisfied with the quality of his officers and implies that, prior to this time, colonels had preferred, or had been obliged by necessity, to assign commissions to men of wealth rather than those with military ability.[26]

If new regiments were raised, rules could change, too. In 1689 when Colonel Riedesel was ordered to raise a new regiment of dragoons, he was allowed to assign officers without obtaining the permission of the elector. Proposals for staff officers and captains had to be submitted to the Elector and *Generalfeldmarschall*, but lieutenants and ensigns could be assigned by the colonel unless the Elector suggested a candidate personally (for example a volunteer).[27]

However, there are also contrary cases of officers – captains and colonels – who used the various deductions from their soldiers' pay to bolster their own income. An audit of the account books of Captain Adam Friedrich von Kospoth from the *Birckholz* dragoons in 1689, after he quit the service, revealed that he had received 941 thalers too much for billeting. It took more than a year to find out where Kospoth was living, and the money was not paid back until 1693.[28]

As already noted the Elector had a preference for men trained in Brandenburg-Prussia. From there the Saxon army recruited many officers, especially during its initial establishment. Officers from this state were

---

23   Thenius, *Die Anfänge des stehenden Heerwesens*, pp. 48–49.
24   *Ibid.*, p. 49.
25   Redlich, *The German Military Enterpriser*, S. 54.
26   Schuster/Francke, *Geschichte der Sächsischen Armee*, p. 113.
27   Thenius, *Die Anfänge des stehenden Heerwesens*, p. 48.
28   See the full record SächsHsta DD 11237-2132.

experienced in war (Brandenburg had recently beaten the redoubtable Swedish army at Fehrbellin) and possessed recruitment networks and organisational capability.

One of the first men to heed John George's call was Colonel Ullrich count von Promnitz. He had commanded a regiment under Montecuccoli in Hungary. As a Protestant he was not able to rise above the rank of colonel in the Habsburg army, so he took service with Friedrich Wilhelm of Brandenburg in 1671 instead and raised a regiment of horse for him. He served against the French on the Rhine and against the Swedes in northern Germany, where he took part in the Battle of Fehrbellin. In 1677 he was promoted to major general. In 1680 he transferred to the Saxon service with the same rank. Promnitz was highly regarded as a soldier and one of the Elector's favourites. Because of his standing within the army, he was also able to draw high-ranking recruits for the officer corps of his regiment, among them his brother Heinrich Count Promnitz and the Duke of Saxe-Zeitz, two members of the regional high nobility.[29]

Family ties often pulled new men into Saxon service. In 1691 the former Brandenburgian officer Heinrich Ehrenreich von Bornstäft became colonel of the Saxon foot guards. Two years later his relative Thomas Friedrich von Bornstädt followed and took command of the cuirassier guards.[30] From the Brandenburgian province of Pomerania the brothers Joachim Rüdiger and Heinrich von der Goltz joined John George's army, as did four members of the family Flemming: Eustachius, Johann Heinrich, Heino Heinrich and in 1693 – after Johann George's death – Jacob Heinrich, who later became the leading man in Saxony during the reign of Augustus the strong.[31] In fact all of John George's general field marshals – von der Goltz, Flemming and Schöning – came directly from the army of Brandenburg.

Family ties were also important for climbing the rank system. When on 21 December 1681 Joachim von Dürfeld, a captain in the cuirassiers, was promoted to lieutenant-colonel, his son Joachim Reinhard took over his old company.[32] On 13 June 1689 Georg Christoph von Minckwitz received a commission as a lieutenant in a company of his father's militia regiment.[33] In the regular infantry, a company of the *Kuffer* Regiment was commanded by the regimental commander's son. This did not save him from arrest in 1686, after he quartered his company in the Duchy of Saxe-Altenburg, in violation of regulations.[34] However, while the records contain examples of this sort of nepotism, it seems that the practice was far from common, and certainly not comparable with the situation in the French army.

While recruits for the rank and file could be hired reasonably easily from within the Electorate and high ranking officers with military experience

29   Anton Balthasar König, *Biographisches Lexikon aller Helden und Militairpersonen.* Band III. (Berlin: Arnold Wever 1791), pp. 237–239; Göse, 'Ressentimentgeladenheit und Rezeptionsbereitschaft', pp. 387–288; Dethloff, *Das kursächsische Offizierskorps*, p. 116.

30   *Ibid.*, p. 388.

31   *Ibid.*, pp 388–389.

32   SächsHsta DD 11237-208, fol. 15.

33   SächsHsta DD 11237-208, fol. 59.

34   SächsHsta DD 11237-884, without fol.

could be obtained from other princes, it was much more difficult to find competent officers of the rank of major and below. These are the men who, together with the NCOs, provide the backbone of any army. One might have expected these posts to have been attractive to Saxon nobles, because military service in general enjoyed a high standing throughout Germany, but for some reason the prestige of being an officer was never as high in Saxony as it was for example in Brandenburg-Prussia.

Nevertheless, there were some Saxon nobles with military experience gained either abroad or in one of the few guard formations of John George II. An unusual example was Hans Hermann Wostromirsky, a descendant of a Lutheran Bohemian noble family which had had to leave the kingdom after the Battle of White Mountain in the Thirty Years' War. Hans Hermann was born in Dresden in 1647 and – according to his own account – attended the Prince School in Grimma from 1660 to 1664, though surviving records do not corroborate this. In 1664 he joined the military as a common musketeer in a regiment of the army of Brunswick-Lüneburg. He learned his profession 'from the pike upwards' (*von der Pike auf*, a saying still in use in Germany today) becoming *Gefreiter* in the company of a Captain Bülau. In 1667 he changed service and joined a Spanish infantry regiment under the command of the Duke of Holstein in Flanders. There he became corporal and served as such for just under two-and-a-half years before becoming an ensign. After the regiment was disbanded in 1670 he crossed the border and took service as *Gefreiter* in a Dutch regiment under Colonel Torsey. Not long after, he became an ensign again in the Königsmarck Regiment. Wostromirsky now slowly climbed the hierarchy. He was promoted to lieutenant in 1672 and captain lieutenant in 1673. From 1676 to 1677 he commanded his own company as captain. He was now an experienced professional and as such was recalled by the reigning Saxon elector John George II as one of his vassals. The Elector promised him his own command, but after the treaty of Nijmwegen was signed, Wostromirsky remained unemployed for three years, receiving nothing but empty promises from his liege lord. It was not until John George III became elector that Wostromirsky received a new command, becoming a captain of the Lifeguards of Foot and an adjutant of the Guards in the residence in 1680. In 1682 he became captain of a Guard company which he commanded during the Vienna campaign and in successive years until 1690 when he received a position as *Oberstwachtmeister* in the *Reuß* Regiment. Wostromirsky pursued a successful career in the Saxon army after John George's death and finally became a brigadier in 1699 and full general of infantry in 1714. He died four years later in the city of his birth after a long and distinguished life of service.[35] His career, especially his start as a common soldier, was unusual even for that time, although not unique. To have men of this calibre in his service was vital for John George.

---

35   Carl Sahrer von Sahr auf Dahlsen, 'Der kursächsische General der Infanterie Wostromürscky von Rockitting', in: Archiv für sächsische Geschichte 5 (1867), pp. 306–318.

A similar example is that of Rudolf von Carlowitz who on 13 June 1685 was promoted from the rank of corporal to the lowest commissioned rank, that of cornet, in a regiment of cuirassiers.[36]

The majority of the officer corps was Lutheran, but Catholics were not automatically rejected. However, when, in 1681, Colonel von Bronne asked to be assigned to the *Kurprinz* Regiment after returning from Imperial service, he was given the advice, that as a Catholic his chances for further advancement would have been better in the Habsburg army.[37]

While it was possible for men from other classes to enter the officer corps, in practice it was dominated by the nobility, which in 1682 made up 90 percent of the total officer corps of 267 men.[38] Their percentage was somewhat higher within the infantry (13 percent) compared to the cavalry (6 percent) but with regard to the low total numbers, one should be careful not to give too much weight to percentages, as individual factors, preferences and the social structures and networks within certain branches are probably more important, than differences between the branches.

A muster roll of the *Kurprinz* Regiment dated 1689 shows all 10 company commanders to be noblemen. A similar list of the Lifeguards of Foot from 1690 shows just one out of 12 captains lacked a title, although five of its 11 lieutenants and three of its 12 ensigns were commoners. This is quite interesting, because the Lifeguards enjoyed an elite status. It is very difficult to establish a reliable percentage for the army in general. In the first *Trützschler* Regiment, all officers were noble, in the *Toppau* Regiment only one in six was non-noble, in the *Kleist* Regiment just one in 15.[39] Presumably candidates of noble birth were preferred, but if there were insufficient to fill the available posts then non-nobles got a chance. However, the higher the rank, the less the likelihood of finding non-nobles there. The only non-noble colonel during John George's reign was Kuffer.

The priority given to the nobility is also evident in the creation of cadet academies to which they had exclusive access. These institutions provided a mixture of military, scientific and classical education. The first was founded by Louis XIV. They were part of the ongoing move towards the creation of professional standing armies and were intended to ensure minimum standards of officer education. Brandenburg created a cadet company in 1686 and this may have influenced Bose to forward a proposal for a Saxon one in 1687. However, the idea for creating such an organisation had existed since the inception of the army and had only failed to get off the ground for want of money. Even after the institution was finally set up in 1692, in the reign of John George IV, officers were still learning their craft on the job.[40]

---

36 SächsHsta DD 11237-208, fol. 37.
37 Thenius, *Die Anfänge des stehenden Heerwesens*, p. 50.
38 Dethloff, *Das kursächsische Offizierskorps*, p. 114.
39 *Ibid.*, pp. 53–54.
40 Thenius, *Die Anfänge des stehenden Heerwesens*, p. 54.

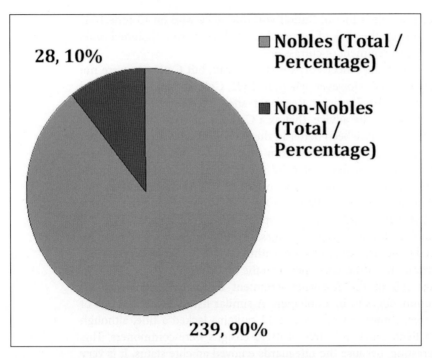

2 Proportion of nobles and non-nobles within the officer corps in 1682.

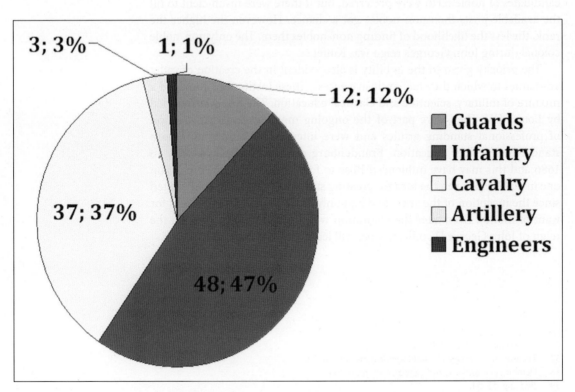

3 Distribution of officers within the branches of the army, 1682.

Table 5. Monthly salaries of Saxon colonels, captains and lieutenants (in thaler)[41]

Year	Colonels			Captains			Lieutenants		
	Cavalry	Dragoons	Infantry	Cavalry	Dragoons	Infantry	Cavalry	Dragoons	Infantry
1682	120	110	100	66	56	44	40	28	20
1688	201	201	186	75	75	54	33	33	21
1689	100	100	80	60	60	40	30	30	18
1692	90	85	80	55	44	36	25	22	17

As can be seen in Table 5, the pay of cavalry officers was about 20 to 30 percent higher than that of infantry officers. In part this was because the prestige of that arm was higher and in part because it needed more training and involved the officers in greater expenditure. Interestingly, the highest remuneration went to the artillery officers. They were normally based at the Main Arsenal in Dresden and were detached as required to command a certain number of guns when the army was on campaign.

Table 6. Payment of artillery officers in the Saxon army, 1682–1691 (in thalers)[42]

Rank / Year	1682	1683	1688	1689	1691
Colonel	200	200	–	200	–
Lieutenant-colonel	100	100	150	150	150
Arsenal captain	–	100	50	60	50
Chief Engineer	56.9	56.21	56.9	56.9	56.9
Engineer	–	30	–	48	48
Arsenal lieutenant	30.6	30.6	–	30	50
Gunner	–	16	16	16	16

---

41   Fritz Redlich, *The German Military Enterpriser and his Work Force. Bd. 2.* (Vierteljahrschrift für Sozial- und Wirtschaftsgeschichte, Beiheft 47) (Wiesbaden: Franz Steiner Verlag 1964), pp. 38, 42.

42   Thenius, *Die Anfänge des stehenden Heerwesens*, p. 47.

5

Rank and File

5.1 Recruitment

The Saxon army, like most European armies of this age, was in fact a permanent army of volunteers, on the Continent generally termed 'mercenaries'. 'Mercenary' does not mean that only foreigners who were in search of profit were recruited; ordinary men – from Saxony or abroad – for whom the small army payment still offered a possibility to subsist also made up the ranks. In fact, most of the troops were of the lower and lowest social classes, but not necessarily 'the scum of the earth'. Regulations of John George II promulgated in the year 1676 stipulated that certain social classes, especially the citizens of towns (this means those, who lived in the 'inner' part of the town, still recognisable by the old medieval walls) craft masters, students and educated men should be more or less exempted. Additionally, the ordinance of 1677 encouraged the recruitment of non-settled, unemployed, unmarried and idle folk.[1] Simply said, the ranks of the units should be filled up with those who were not fully integrated into society. This protected the economy and gave cash to those, who otherwise filled the streets as beggars. This thinking fitted in perfectly with contemporary theories of mercantilism and centralisation. Surprisingly, even though the social standing of soldiers was low, the promise of food and shelter in addition to wages even resonated with those in employment, because such men had to provide their own sustenance.

In the event that new units were required or additional recruits were looked for, the Elector presented an officer with a recruiting warrant. This would be a colonel if a complete regiment was to be raised, a captain in the case of a company, or a sergeant if just replenishment was needed. The warrant assigned them to a certain area, in most cases a complete circle or province or – if troops were being hired from abroad – another principality. The recruiting officers had to report to the regional or local officials and show their authority signed by the Elector. After that, they should be aided by the locals in every possible way.[2]

---

1   Dietzel, 'Zur Militärverfassung', pp. 439–440.
2   Thenius, *Die Anfänge des stehenden Heerwesens*, p. 65.

However, many complaints about recruitment were registered. In May 1689 for example the municipal council of Laubau wrote to the Alderman of Upper Lusatia in Bautzen and told him, that the one sergeant's recruitment squad was not only operating during the weekly markets, but also on Sundays and holidays so that the populations of the nearby villages were now too afraid to venture into town.[3]

It was not unknown for Saxon recruiting officers to use force, or scams, to achieve their ends. For example in August 1687 an Andreas Küchler complained, that, while on a trip to Leipzig, 'his son Samuel … was dragged from his coach by the men of Captain Alenbeck [of the *Löben* Regiment], treated to a bloody beating and forcibly enlisted.'[4]

However, cheating men into service was not welcome, because these men tended to undermine discipline and to desert. Because of that, the mandate of 1682 clearly forbade recruiting by force, getting men drunk or using other tricks. On the other hand, it also forbade the discharge of recruits in return for payment. Recruiting officers were asked to take care not to take the sons of citizens and peasants if they were dependent on their labour. If a man was recruited illegally he should be released contingent upon his repaying the shilling he had received at the time of enlistment.[5] In the case of Samuel Küchler it was decided, 'because he had been recruited illegally, not only should he be released from service immediately, but also those who mistreated him [should be] strictly punished.'[6] Similarly, three years later Tobias Schmidt from the mining town Johanngeorgenstadt begged that his son should be discharged, because he was a miner's mate. In this case, the War Council ordered, that he be discharged 'without reward or impression of another position.'[7]

This 'shilling' could vary, depending on the financial resources of the state and of the recruitment party and also of the capacity of the potential recruit. Normally it ranged from two to 20 thaler, but trained experts were paid even more, so 25 thalers for an arsenal servant and 48 for a master gunner.[8]

There was no fixed period of service; each recruit entered into an individual contract between himself and the army. The latter was interested in engaging good men for a long time: 8 to 10 years in the infantry and 10 to 15 in the cavalry.[9]

Shortly after he came to power, John George III forbade Saxons from enlisting in foreign armies. Up until that time Austria and Prussia in particular had obtained many men from the Electorate. Just how important this matter was to the Elector may be inferred from the fact that more than 2,000 copies of his decree on the subject were printed.[10] The secundogeniture dukes objected, arguing, officially, that only they were allowed to publish

---

3   *Ibid.*, pp. 65–66.
4   Quot.: SächsHsta DD 11237-886, without fol.
5   Mandat über die Neuordnung des Militärwesens im Kurfürstentum Sachsen, January 1682.
6   Quot.: SächsHsta DD 11237-886, without fol.
7   Quot.: *Ibid.*
8   Thenius, *Die Anfänge des stehenden Heerwesens*, p. 66.
9   *Ibid.*, p. 66.
10   *Ibid.*, p. 69.

such orders, but their real reason for objecting was that they were being paid considerable sums by Austria and Brandenburg-Prussia to allow recruiting. The practice must have continued surreptitiously because John George republished his decree in 1685 and 1688, and in 1685 he also signed an agreement with the elector of Brandenburg-Prussia in which the two men undertook to refrain from recruiting in the other's territory.[11]

Recruiting was not easy for officers, especially in Saxony, which had a well developed economy and where employment rates were high. A decree issued in 1682 illustrates the point: officers were not to hire craftsmen, because many cities had complained about the practice.[12]

As might be expected, recruitment for the Saxon army in the secundogeniture duchies proved to be a headache. While the burden on them was no higher than in the hereditary lands, the Dukes were always trying to evade their responsibilities by making exaggerated claims to 'sovereignty'. Christian of Saxe-Merseburg not only forbade recruitment in his territory, he even arrested men recruited for Saxon service in the summer of 1687. On the other hand the Dukes sometimes raised recruits themselves and sold them to the Austrian army, against the protests of the Elector, who argued that he needed the men himself.[13]

With the beginning of the Nine Years' war in 1688 there was an increased demand for soldiers all over Europe. Recruiting officers had problems filling the ranks. To make the service more attractive, payment was temporarily increased (see Table 7), but this failed to provide all the men needed so recruitment by force also increased, as is indicated by the number of letters of protest in the records, especially for the years 1689 and 1690.[14]

Table 7 Soldier's monthly wages (in thalers)[15]

	1682	1683	1688	1690	1692
Cavalry	5	4⅔	6	4⅔	4⅔
Dragoons	4	4	6	4	4
Infantry	2½	2½	3	2½	2½

The age of seventeenth and eighteenth century soldiers was higher than that of nineteenth and twentieth century recruits. Normally about a third were older than 30. For example, during the 1683 campaign, Kuffer's infantry regiment had 303 men older than 30 within its ranks. One hundred and eleven were older than 40, 18 even older than 50.[16]

The militia was not yet a recruiting pool for the army. The idea was being considered, but the bad discipline of the militiamen made it unattractive. On

11 *Ibid.*, p. 69.
12 Mandat über die Neuordnung des Militärwesens im Kurfürstentum Sachsen, January 1682.
13 Thenius, *Die Anfänge des stehenden Heerwesens*, p. 23.
14 Compare; SächsHsta DD 11237-886, without fol.; SächsHsta DD 11237-884, without fol.
15 Redlich, *The German Military Enterpriser*, S. 244. See also SächsHsta DD 10024-13541/35, without fol.
16 Hassel / Vitzthum von Eckstädt, *Zur Geschichte des Türkenkrieges*, pp. 117–118.

30 October 1690, Haugwitz wrote to the elector: 'There are fewer complaints about the whole standing army than about the militia; and if we build up the standing army by employing militiamen, complaints about it, too, will increase.'[17]

An additional way of raising the strength of the Saxon army was by obtaining the services of tiny contingents of neighbouring territories. Just as the Dutch filled up their army by hiring foreign, especially German, troops, so the bigger German principalities tried to strengthen their control over the small forces of the estates around them. The princes of Anhalt-Dessau for example maintained their own regiment in the army of Brandenburg-Prussia. Electoral Saxony was always interested in winning political control over the territories in Thuringia which were ruled by the older, but now less powerful, branch of the Ernestins. Getting control of their military was part of Dresden's plan to achieve hegemony in the region. As early as 1669 John George II had been in correspondence with the secundogenitures about a defensive alliance that would include their Ernestin cousins. However, the Thuringian dukes were always jealous of the electoral line – they would never forget the loss of this title – and were, with good reason, suspicious about the political and maybe even territorial ambitions of Dresden. It was expected that the Saxe-Altenburg line would die out sooner rather than later. The two older lines of Saxe-Weimar and Saxe-Gotha wanted to rearrange the territory within the Ernestin branch. However, fears were high that electoral Saxony would stake out a claim to the duchy, which was sited temptingly next to its western border. The Dukes concluded that giving the Elector control of their military would seriously weaken their position so the proposed alliance with Dresden was dropped. This in turn meant the idea of an inter-Ernestin confederation was also dropped. Without a strong partner it made no sense.[18]

New negotiations were started after France declared war on the Dutch Republic and threatened the border of the Empire, but, although the representatives of the various parties drew up an agreement, it was never ratified. The Dukes did agree, however, that in the case of war with France they would integrate their forces into the electoral army. Dresden benefited also from the Imperial war constitution, which divided the Empire into administrative areas. The Saxon elector was head of the Upper Saxon area. When the Empire declared war on France in 1674 the Ernestin contingents, consisting of a squadron of horse (80 men) and two companies of infantry (120 men each) were integrated into the Saxon army. The infantry companies were attached to the electoral Lifeguards regiment and the troopers formed part of a circle regiment of horse (*Kreisregiment zu Pferd*) under the command of Prince Heinrich von Sachsen-Gotha. Until the treaty of Nimwegen the Thuringian troops served under electoral command.[19]

---

17   Thenius, *Die Anfänge des stehenden Heerwesens*, p. 64.
18   Oliver Heyn, 'Die Ernestiner und die Reichsdefension', in: Werner Greiling a.o. (ed.), *Die Ernestiner. Politik, Kultur und gesellschaftlicher Wandel* (Veröffentlichungen der Historischen Kommission für Thüringen, Kleine Reihe 50) (Köln – Weimar – Wien: Böhlau Verlag 2016), pp. 185–204, here pp. 188–189.
19   *Ibid.*, pp. 190–191.

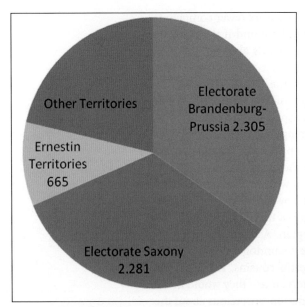

Other Territories

Ernestin Territories 665

Electorate Brandenburg-Prussia 2.305

Electorate Saxony 2.281

4 Proportion of the territories of the Upper Saxon Circle for the Simplum of the Imperial Army 1681.

As a result of the Dutch War, the Imperial war constitution was reformed in 1681/82. It now required the Upper Saxon Circle to provide 1,322 cavalry and 2,707 infantry. A circle diet in Leipzig in November 1681 established the Ernestin contingent at 131 troopers and 267 infantry. However, despite this attempt to improve the effectiveness of Imperial forces, the Upper Saxon Circle was rendered impotent by the rivalry between Saxony and Brandenburg and this state of affairs continued until the break-up of the Empire in 1806. The congress in Leipzig in 1681 was the last assembly of the circle estates. After that the smaller states, like the Ernestin dukedoms, were obliged to form separate alliances with strong neighbours, if they wished to survive. In 1680 Saxe-Weimar, Saxe-Gotha-Altenburg and Saxe-Eisenach were the principal branches of the Ernestin dynasty, but with the death of Ernst the Pious, Saxe-Gotha-Altenburg split into six lines, the junior branches except for Saxe-Meiningen being still subordinate to Saxe-Gotha. The ambitions of the new duke, Fredrick I of Saxe-Gotha, pushed the Saxe-Weimar branch into the arms of the Elector, and an alliance was signed in 1682. Just how far jealousy and mutual recrimination could go now became apparent as Saxe-Eisenach and Saxe-Gotha, instead of following the example of Saxe-Weimar, went off and joined the Franconian and Upper Rhine circles, turning the complex but well-thought-out Imperial defence system into chaos. The so-called Frankfurt Alliance extended in June 1682 to the Laxenburg Alliance of which the Emperor was part. Troops of this alliance took part in the battle of Vienna, so contingents of Saxe-Einseach fought as part of the Franconian Circle forces, while troops from Weimar formed part of John George III's army.[20]

In 1685 the Laxenburg Alliance was replaced by the Augsburg Alliance, for which the Ernestins wanted to raise a complete regiment of infantry of 1,000 men. However, because the bigger armed estates did not join this confederation, it fell to another to raise the forces to oppose Louis XIV's invasion of the Palatinate in 1688. The Ernestins did not join this group, known as the Magdeburger Concert, but instead signed a separate alliance with electoral Saxony on 13 May 1689. In fact, there were two alliances, one between Saxe-Gotha-Altenburg and the Electorate and the other between Saxe-Weimar and Saxe-Eisenach and the electorate. In total, the Dukes promised to raise a cavalry regiment of 390 men and two infantry regiments of 800 men each and these units accompanied John George's army to Würzburg that summer. This so-called Leipziger alliance was intended to last just three years but was prolonged by Saxe-Weimar and Saxe-Eisenach after John

---

20   Heyn, 'Die Ernestiner und die Reichsdefension', pp. 191–192. See also: Heyn, *Das Militär des Fürstentums Sachsen-Hildburghausen*, pp. 293–295.

George's death in 1692. As already noted, at this time Saxe-Gotha-Altenburg became split between six branches of that family and because the new duke of the premier line was under age and stood under the tutelage of the Saxe-Meiningen and Saxe-Römhild branches, the duchy fell once again under the influence of the Franconian Circle.[21] This probably did not worry the Elector unduly because, in 1691, he negotiated a contract with Saxe-Gotha in which the duchy undertook to supply him with two 1,000-man infantry regiments for three years. In return, Saxony paid Gotha 25,000 thalers each year.[22]

5.2 NCOs and Ordinary Men

In the aftermath of the Thirty Years' War the commissioned and non-commissioned officers became more and more destinctivly separated, not just hierarchically, but also socially. While in the sixteenth and early seventeenth century it was not uncommon that nobles made their way through the NCO ranks, they now stood in a more or less closed circle within the CO ranks. However, there were also exceptions to the rule. In the cavalry regiment *Promnitz* in 1680 all NCOs were nobles,[23] but this example is more suitable to demonstrate a certain difference in the social composition between cavalry and infantry units. In the case, that NCO positions were filled with nobles, they could also be passed on within one family. For example on 4 March 1682 Friedrich Otto von Carstädt followed his father as a corporal.[24]

The highest of the old NCO ranks was that of the *Feldwebel*. This German term became unpopular in the second half of the century and was replaced with the French *Sergeant*. Sometimes both terms were used, the *Feldwebel* still being higher, like a 1st Sergeant in modern systems. In Saxony the term *Feldwebel* was used until the reign of John George II. Under his son it was completely replaced by *Sergeant*. This officer was responsible for the company books, the equipment of the unit and the drilling of the men. Orders from the COs to the men were given through him. It is interesting to notice that in 1692, the year after John George III's death, the *Feldwebel* again could be found in regimental lists. Beneath this (unofficial) 'first' sergeant there were two more in each company.[25]

For the daily routine and duties, the company was divided into three commands, led by a corporal. He had to inspect the equipment of the men and report shortcomings to the sergeants, and detail tasks and guards. His weapon was a bullpup rifle.[26]

The *Gefreitenkorporal* was an assistant to the ensign and had to carry the colours during the march, as the ensign only did it ceremonially and in battle. Most companies had a clerk for the paperwork, assisting the sergeants,

---

21 Heyn, 'Die Ernestiner und die Reichsdefension', pp. 193–194.
22 SächsHsta DD 10024-9088/13, fol. 106.
23 Thenius, *Die Anfänge des stehenden Heerwesens*, p. 61.
24 SächsHsta DD 11237-208, fol. 205. It is not known in which regiment he did so.
25 Thenius, *Die Anfänge des stehenden Heerwesens*, p. 58.
26 *Ibid.*, p. 59.

lieutenants and captains in their respective jobs. In 1687 John George ordered their abolition, to reduce costs, however most companies kept them in office. The *Capitän d'armes*, despite his name, was an NCO also and was responsible for guns and spare uniforms and equipment. Very important was the *fourier*, who had to distribute rations, provide quarters with the help of the commissars and on campaign laid out the camp ground together with the regimental quartermaster. A feldsher (*Feldscher*) per company was also an NCO.[27]

The *Gefreite* (comparable to a modern private first class) did not belong to the NCOs, but were ranked a little higher than common soldiers. They did not have to do sentinel guard duties, nor take care for arrestees and could act as orderlies for staff officers.[28]

Payment standards were lower, compared to the Landsknecht period of the sixteenth century. Additionally, wages were reduced by deductions for uniforms, weapons and social care. Deductions for uniforms ranged from 8 to 12 groschen for the main dress and a further eight for small uniform items (*Beimontur* = shirts, neckcloth, stockings, shoes, gloves), administered by the lieutenant-colonel in the first and the major in the second battalion. If a man died or was disbanded and his uniform or parts of it were still serviceable, he (or his heirs) received a share of his deductions back.[29]

The cavalry units also had a horse coffer (*Pferdekasse*), to which each trooper contributed a further eight groschen. From this coffer veterinary costs were paid. If a horse was wounded or otherwise unfit, the colonel could give the trooper money to pay for a veterinarian. If it was killed in battle the *Kriegszahlamt* paid for the new horse (*Remontierungsgelder*).[30]

Finally, weapons were also paid for from the soldiers' wages. This seemed necessary to force the men to conserve their equipment. The regulations of 1687 lamented in their introduction that the cavalry in paticular always left behind a considerable amount of weaponrys when bivouacs were broken up. In 1691 Bose reported to the Elector that there were regiments which lacked up to 20 muskets and 125 cartridge boxes per company! Also the *Schweinsfedern* seemed to 'get lost' easily. Because of this sloppy dealing with weapons, the state had to use more money for re-equipping the units which in turn went on the expense of provisions. Because the officers were responsible for weapons, the deductions would be taken from their payment.

Additionally 11 thalers were collected from all the troopers. The common men in the infantry officially did not had to pay money for guns, however, many captains tried to regain their deductions from their men's wages. The collections of *Gewehrgelder* as described in the table above were not taken during John George's reign; it was not until the reign of his son Augustus that this money was collected and then it was also taken from the common men's wages.[31]

---

27 *Ibid.*, p. 59–60.
28 *Ibid.*, p. 61.
29 *Ibid.*, p. 82.
30 August von Minckwitz, 'Die wirtschaftlichen Einrichtungen namentlich die Verpflegungs-Verhältnisse bei der kursächsischen Kavallerie vom Jahre 1680 bis zum Anfang des laufenden Jahrhunderts', in: *NASG* 2 (1881), pp. 312–329, here p. 13.
31 Thenius, *Die Anfänge des stehenden Heerwesens*, p. 84.

Table 8 Deductions for weapons (in thaler)

Rank	Infantry	Cavalry
Captain	10	15
Lieutenant	3	4
Ensign	2	3
Wachtmeister (2 in each cav. comp.) Sergeant (3 in each inf. comp.)	3	2
Unteroffiziere (4 in each inf. comp.)	5 th 8 groschen	
Corporals (3 in each cav. comp., 4 in each inf. comp)	1 th 16 gr.	3
Fourier		2

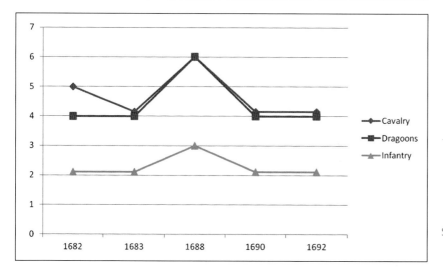

5 Payment of common Soldiers 1682–1692. (Thenius, *Die Anfänge des stehenden Heerwesens*, p. 106)

The graph above shows the development of the payment of soldiers. Generally cuirassiers and dragoons earned nearly twice the money of ordinary soldiers (4.16 thalers or 4 thaler) compared to 2.12 thaler. There is a very interesting increase of around 50 percent in 1688, the year the Nine Years' War broke out. This increase is a remarkable proof of the fact, that the army had to convince recruits by offering good payment instead of forcing or cheating them into service. The Nine Years' War affected nearly all of central and western Europe so the demand for recruits on the 'soldier market' far exceeded supply and armies had to offer better payment if they did not want to lose men to competitors. This also underlines the voluntary aspect of service, compared to the traditional view of seventeenth and eighteenth century soldiers as unwilling men controlled by force.

Payment was given out every 10 days. The already low pay, especially for the infantry, was further reduced by deductions, amounting to 1 thaler 14 groschen, cutting the common musketeer's payment to less than half![32]

32 *Ibid.*, pp. 109–110.

5.3 Discipline

Putting forces on a permanent footing did not eliminate the problems of the early modern mercenary system. The army of John George consisted to a great degree of foreigners with no connection to the Saxon population. And even those hired from within a country surely had not just been dissocialised rascals but members of lower classes who had not been able to integrate fully into their own communities. The army offered a new home for them and it could easily be guessed, that they regarded the members of their former circles who had been successful in civilian life with a kind of jealousy.

All this made for bigger and smaller troubles in the civilian–military relationship. Already in 1683 John George had to notice with regret 'that in our military, especially in the cavalry and the regiment of dragoons all kinds of disorders insolencies and excesses are going on by not alone ruining their horses but riding back and forth inflicting damage to the grain in the fields, and otherwise causing many mischiefs and complaints.'[33] The damaging of crops by riding through the fields seems to have been a popular if childish sport by horsemen, because similar charges could be found en masse during the Thirty Years' War. The same published mandate charged cavalry units for robbing the horses of travellers and merchants.[34]

A more serious problem were the constant rampages of soldiers against their hosts. Ralf Pröve has argued, that problems like these had been teething problems of early modern armies.[35] This seems plausible for the Saxon army of this time too. The regiments had no permanent garrisons, were often on campaign and received new quarters when they came back, so there was no time to tighten personal relations to a certain community. All the mandates published in the name of John George III which could improve the situation start with charges against his own military and so prove that the complaints of the populations were not ignored.

To the contrary, the 1682 mandate demanded in its first paragraph, 'In the case that it [the quarter] is neither good for officers or men they have to complain to government authorities and not act on their own will and authority.'[36] Point two forbade them to take or demand money instead of or in addition to their quarters. Point four exempted the nobility and their

---

33 Orig.: 'daß bey Unserer Miliz, absonderlich bei der Reutherey und dem Regiment Dragoner allerhand disordren insolentien und excesse vorgehen indem sie nicht allein mit hin und wieder reuthen ihre pferde verderben im felde dem Getreyde Schaden zufügen und sonst allerhand Unheil und Klagen verursachen.' Quot: Mandat Johann Georgs III. gegen Militärexzesse, 8. Dezember 1683.

34 Ibid.

35 Pröve has studied the mandates against this kind of excesses in the Hannoverian army and found that their number decreased dramatically in the middle of the eighteenth century, which to him is a proof of better civilian-military relations in the quarters making the permanent republishing of mandates obsolete, see: Ralf Pröve, 'Der Soldat in der "guten Bürgerstube". Das frühneuzeitliche Einquartierungssystem und die sozioökonomischen Folgen', in: Bernard R.Kroener/Ralf Pröve (ed.) Krieg und Frieden. Militär und Gesellschaft in der Frühen Neuzeit (Paderborn e.a.: Ferdinand Schoeningh 1996), pp. 191–217, here pp. 196–200.

36 Quot.: Mandat über die Neuordnung des Militärwesens im Kurfürstentum Sachsen, January 1682.

estates, university professors, churches and school teachers from quartering. Point six made it absolutely clear that in addition to quarter, only salt, pepper, vinegar, light (candles), wood and a bed should be provided and 'more not demanded'.[37] However, instead of this small service money could be paid, see Table 9.

Table 9 Accommodation allowance for small service according to the *Mandat über die Table 9) Neuordnung des Militärwesens im Kurfürstentum Sachsen*, January 1682[38]

Horseman		Dragoon		Musketeer	
Service	Money (in groschen and Pfennige)	Service	Money	Service	Money
Salt	1 Gr. 7 Pf.	Salt	1 Gr. 4 Pf.	Salt	1 Gr. 3 Pf.
Pepper	1 Gr. 7 Pf.	Pepper	1 Gr. 4 Pf.	Pepper	1 Gr. 3 Pf.
Vinegar	2 Gr. 2 Pf.	Vinegar	2 Gr.	Vinegar	1 Gr. 6 Pf.
Light	2 Gr. 8 Pf.	Light	2 gr. 3 Pf.	Light	1 Gr. 9 Pf.
Wood	2 Gr. 9 Pf.	Wood	2 Gr. 4 Pf.	Wood	1 Gr. 9 Pf.
Bed	3 Gr. 3 Pf.	Bed	2 gr. 9 Pf.	Bed	2 Gr. 6 Pf.
Total	**14 gr.**	**Total**	**12 Gr.**	**Total**	**10 Gr.**

The soldier was also free to decide to take another quarter. In this case, his host had to pay him money, but not more than 12 groschen.[39] Many soldiers took this money, spent a part of it on cheaper (and generally worse) quarters and kept the rest for themselves, so this system offered them a new chance for additional income.

However, problems with quartering were not one sided. On 21 March 1682 the Elector sent an order to all administrative bodies, that the 1682 ordinance had to be followed immediately (*schnurstracks*) and that subjects who disobeyed this demands should be put in jail. But the same order reminded the soldiers not to take anything by force, if it was not given to them, even if they had a right to their claim.[40]

Many troubles arose, because soldiers were hungry and demanded food from their hosts or other suppliers in a city. There is an interesting instance of six soldiers from the infantry regiment *Kuffer*, who on 8 November 1684 stopped a baker at the Grimma Gate of Leipzig (a city with comparably high living costs), took three loaves of bread and wanted to pay with 18 pennies each, while the baker demanded two shillings for one. He rejected the payment. The men argued that they were hungry, so they left without paying him at all. On the same day another group of 15 soldiers robbed a baker on the other side of the city. The man did not want to give them the bread, because he was not allowed to sell it outside the city walls. On the other

37   Quot.: *Mandat über die Neuordnung des Militärwesens im Kurfürstentum Sachsen*, January 1682.
38   SächsHsta DD 11237-463, fol. 18–19.
39   Thenius, *Die Anfänge des stehenden Heerwesens*, p. 85.
40   SächsHsta DD 11237-463, fol. 45.

hand the soldiers were not allowed to enter the city, because it was free from billeting. The Elector reacted and answered the complaints of the magistrate with a letter from 11 November, in which he ordered them to take care that a bakery in the suburbs should provide enough payable bread for the soldiers.[41] This incidents make clear once more, that compliants of civilians and soldiers alike were considered serious and that the early modern state did not react immediately with draconian punishment, but tried to solve problems.

In 1683 the city of Grimma lamented many crimes committed by soldiers of the infantry regiment *Löben*. Interestingly, they made the senior officers of the regiment responsible, who were 'rarely located here'.[42] Their absence from the regiment caused lax discipline.

Officers had to pay for their quarters, but could claim comparably for a lot of room. According to the supplement of the 1682 mandate, a colonel could demand two rooms for himself and one for his servants, and stables for 12 (cavalry) or 10 (infantry horses). A lieutenant-colonel was allowed two rooms for himself and servants plus stables for 10 and eight horses respectively, a major two rooms and stables for eight or six horses, captains one room and place for six or four horses.[43]

On marches the men should receive food against payment, namely for horsemen and musketeers half a pound of meat, a pot of beer and a pound of bread for one groschen. For a further 1 groschen 3 Pfennige a 'Dresdner Metze' (approx. 6.4 litres) of oats and six pounds of hay should be provided for horses. NCOs and officers received more.[44]

The mandate also contained a list of things forbidden to officers and soldiers, implying that these crimes were not uncommon at the time. They were not allowed to mow grain or take anything from meadows and gardens, or force people to sell it to them. Hunting and fishing were also forbidden. Only the colonels were allowed to have dogs for hunting but they also should respect the electoral reveres (hunting grounds).[45] However, the mandate of 1686 noted that officers frequently sent their musketeers fishing or sent their men out hunting rabbits and chickens and that lower grade officers also kept their own dogs. The mandate invited the colonels to take care that no dogs were maintained and no illegal hunting executed.[46]

Another crime committed by soldiers was highway robbery, reported to be undertaken by parts of the cavalry. In 1686 the Elector published a mandate which demanded that soldiers had to stay in the villages assigned as their quarters and were not allowed to leave them without a pass signed by their officer. Guards had to be posted on the roads and if a soldier left his quarter, the host had to report this to an officer.[47] This last point is impressive

---

41   SächsHsta DD 11237-884, without fol., report of the magistrate from 4 November, answer of John George III. from the 11th.

42   Quot.: SächsHsta DD 11237-886, without fol.

43   Thenius, *Die Anfänge des stehenden Heerwesens*, p. 86.

44   Mandat über die Neuordnung des Militärwesens im Kurfürstentum Sachsen, January 1682.

45   Mandat über die Neuordnung des Militärwesens im Kurfürstentum Sachsen, January 1682.

46   Mandat 1686, § 6.

47   Mandat Johann Georgs III. gegen Militärexzesse, 8. Dezember 1683; SächsHstA Dresden 11237/464 Gedruckte Mandata, ohne Bl..

proof that the quartering of soldiers in civilian houses required reciprocal military–civilian monitoring. While the soldier represented the executive arm of the Elector – especially in a time with no police forces – the host had to take care that his guest would not desert.

While the excesses performed by Saxon soldiers in this time stressed their relationship to the civilian population, and in individual cases was brutal and serious, they definitely represented the teething problems of a newly established army. The publication of many mandates concerning these crimes show that the state was willing to fix the problems and restore order. They were necessary steps of a vernier-type adjustment based on recent experiences, made to optimise the military juggernaut.

Outside the Electorate troops could be volatile. There is a sharp contrast between the many complaints of Imperial commissaries and the praise of the Venetian general capitain Francesco Morosoni, who said the Saxons distinguished themselves from all others by their good discipline.[48]

There seems to be an obvious explanation for this. The provision of Saxon troops when fighting for the Emperor against the French or the Ottomans always caused tensions between Dresden and Vienna. While the Saxons argued that they did their duty by sending troops and that their new 'employer' had to care for them (so that the own budget would be relieved), the Imperialists were somewhat over-challenged to organise an effective distribution of supplies for all the small contingents of Imperial princes and circles, and so demanded that they organise it themselves, at least on their route to the front. This conflict was carried out on the backs – or better said, the stomachs – of the common soldiers, so it seems plausible that they felt forced from time to time to look out for themselves. Regarding this, excesses seem to be the product not of a general ill discipline of the troops but of administrative failures. This is underlined by the much better conduct of the Saxons when in Venetian service, where their provisions were paid for by the Serenissima.

Desertion was another typical and constant problem for the army. However, some distinct reasons could be identified. It has already been shown that a majority of the recruits were volunteers for whom the army was an attractive employer, especially during peacetime. But the threats of war and the possibility of being injured and killed, or suffering through disease, reduced this attractiveness. When the infantry regiment *Kurprinz* set out for Austria in 1688, 61 men deserted. The Saxon army in this time never operated alone but always with other allies, some of which offered much better conditions of service. This seems to have been the main reason for the departure of 40 men who left the *Kurprinz* regiment in October 1689 for Dutch service. However, during a campaign, especially in Hungary, the desertion rate was comparably low. The Lifeguards of Foot lost fewer than six men through desertion in October 1690 in Hungary. It seems that those who were willing to leave did so before the start of a campaign or during quartering

---

48   Friesen, 'Feldzüge in Morea 1685 u. 1686', p. 246.

(which was also the time when foreign recruiting officers were more active), while during a campaign or siege few men fled from the colours.[49]

Another common crime, common to officers and men alike, was duelling. Fighting for honour could also lead to desertion. So in 1684 two corporals of the *Löben* infantry regiment fought a duel. One was killed and while his body was brought into the garrison town, 'the committer soon afterwards became invisible.'[50] The fear of harsh punishment for one crime led the survivors of duels to commit another.

Military law provided for death as punishment for desertion. However, this sentence was seldom enforced. Instead, fortification labour, the gauntlet, or exile were more common.[51]

5.4 Jurisdiction

Already in 1672 John George II had published a mandate ordering the separation of military and civilian justice with the exception of cases of debt. The army mandate of 1682 put jurisdiction into the hands of the colonels of the individual regiments.[52] This still resembles practices of the 'golden age' of mercenary forces in the sixteenth and early seventeenth century. There was no codified general military law at this time, this only came under Frederick August I.

However, some general contract letters for each of the services had been published, cavalry in 1664, infantry in 1673 and artillery in 1654, renewed in 1673, describing general behaviours. Quite interesting is the demand in the infantry contract, that soldiers should retain a peaceful commerce with comrades of another religious confession, demonstrating that the army even in a confessionally very strict country like Saxony was open to all Christians.[53] Two special contracts for the Lifeguards and the garrison in Dresden were published in 1684 and 1686.

Minor punishments could be imposed by the captain. The lieutenant and the ensign were not allowed to punish the men themselves. Other crimes had to be reported by the captain to the major first.[54]

Late in 1683, after he came back from the Battle of Vienna, complaints from Austria reached John George. The Imperials lamented the heavy excesses of Saxon troops in Bohemia. They had left their route of march, pressed money, stolen cattle, set fires, and even robbed churches. The Elector started an inquiry of his commanders, who all rejected the charges. Just one detachment had left its route, because it was not usable. Changing its direction, the detachment was not able to find provisions. The alleged church robbery would have been nothing more than the breaking into of a locked

---

49   Thenius, *Die Anfänge des stehenden Heerwesens*, p. 118.
50   Quot.: SächsHsta DD 11237-886, without fol.
51   Thenius, *Die Anfänge des stehenden Heerwesens*, pp. 118–119.
52   Mandat über die Neuordnung des Militärwesens im Kurfürstentum Sachsen, January 1682.
53   Thenius, *Die Anfänge des stehenden Heerwesens*, pp. 112–114.
54   *Ibid.*, p. 56.

Plate 1 Senior Officer of Cavalry *c.* 1680.
(Illustration by Sergey Shamenkov, © Helion & Company 2019)
See Colour Plate Commentaries for further information

Plate 2 Infantry Officer, 1680s.
(Illustration by Sergey Shamenkov, © Helion & Company 2019)
See Colour Plate Commentaries for further information

Plate 3 Cavalry Trooper, *c*. 1680.
(Illustration by Sergey Shamenkov, © Helion & Company 2019)
See Colour Plate Commentaries for further information

Plate 4 Gunner, *c*. 1680.
(Illustration by Sergey Shamenkov, © Helion & Company 2019)
See Colour Plate Commentaries for further information

Plate 5 Musketeer, *Leibregiment zu Fuss*, Guards Infantry Regiment in 1680.
(Illustration by Sergey Shamenkov, © Helion & Company 2019)
See Colour Plate Commentaries for further information

Plate 6 Musketeer Regiment *von Kuffer* in 1680.
(Illustration by Sergey Shamenkov, © Helion & Company 2019)
See Colour Plate Commentaries for further information

Plate 7A Musketeer, Regiment *Sachsen-Weissenfels*.
Plate 7B Musketeer, Regiment *von Löben*.
(Illustration by Sergey Shamenkov, © Helion & Company 2019)
See Colour Plate Commentaries for further information

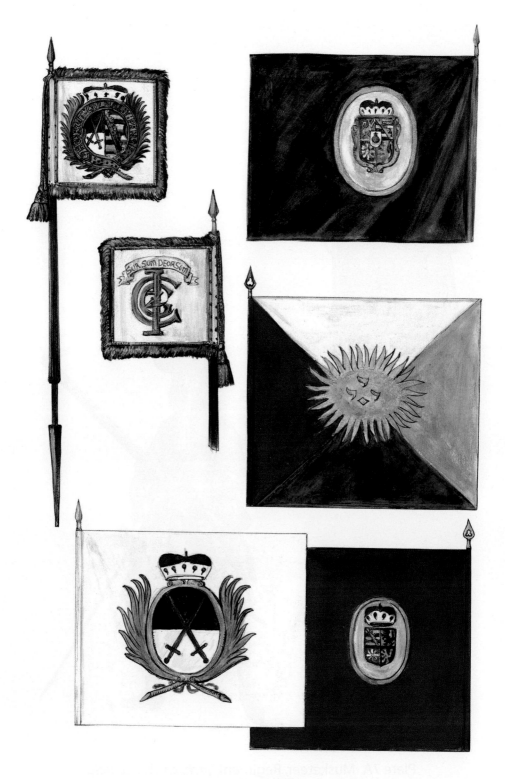

Plate 8 Saxon Colours.
(Illustration by Sergey Shamenkov, © Helion & Company 2019)
See Colour Plate Commentaries for further information

church, where bread was kept. This would not have been necessary if the Imperial commissaries had done their duty, instead of causing so much trouble to all the Saxon troops marching to the relief of Vienna. This answer together with a formal apology was forwarded to the Emperor by John George, who also wrote to him, that he would investigate the charges further and punish the guilty delinquents.[55]

The manifold ways of recruiting troops, especially the hiring of complete foreign units, complicated a uniform jurisdiction. When John George signed his contract with the Ernestins in Leipzig in 1689, who promised to provide one cavalry and two infantry regiments, both units were allowed to stay under their own jurisdiction.

Punishment could be strict. However, according to the laws of the time, it could also be regarded as merciful. While deserters could be hanged, many were sentenced to fortress labour or the gauntlet. Early modern law wanted to punish the crime, not the criminal. Playing dice for their lives to give every second convict a pardon was a common practice of the Landsknecht era. When during the 1683 campaign four musketeers were sentenced to death for plundering, they played for their lives.[56] The two winners were free, the third man was hanged, but the fourth received a pardon from the Elector.[57] This mix of gambling and granted pardons (mostly through appeal by senior officers) was typical for military law till the eighteenth century. The same was done to more than 30 men sentenced to death for fleeing the battlefield of Fraustadt in 1706.

5.5 Daily Life

The Saxon army had no barracks at this time. Only a few were constructed in fortresses. Königstein, for example, had one of the oldest barracks in Germany, but they were only used for the small garrison company.

The majority of infantry and cavalry were billeted in the quarters of citizens. On 28 January 1682 the Elector published a statute (*Mandat*) considering the billeting of the troops. The soldiers received billets (*Quartierscheine*) and so were quartered in the houses of citizens and villagers. These additionally had to offer them salt, pepper, vinegar, light (candles), wood and a bed. The same bill regulated recruitment and warned officers, that nobodu '[unable to] present a patent will presume himself to it nor force the people into war service by drinking other forbidden ways or threat.'[58] It also warned officers, especially of the infantry, not to employ butchers underhand or pay them, when they buy stolen livestock without paying the penny on meat, which was to the disadvantage of the electoral tax.[59] This warning just proves that

---

55   Karl Gustav Helbig, 'Kurfürst Johann Georg der Dritte in seinen Beziehungen zum Kaiser und zum Reich 1682 und 1683', in: *Archiv für Sächsische Geschichte* 9 (1871), pp. 79–110, here p. 108.

56   Thenius, *Die Anfänge des stehenden Heerwesens*, p. 123.

57   SächsHsta DD 11237-10812/15, fol. 11.

58   Vgl.: SächsHsta Dresden 11237/464 Gedruckte Mandata, ohne Bl.

59   Vgl.: SächsHsta Dresden 11237/464 Gedruckte Mandata, ohne Bl.

this practice was very common within the army and that officers tried to save money by cheating the state and not only by neglecting the quality of the provisions for their men. Another problem emerged through the common practice of exacting money instead of the rations the hosts had to offer to the soldiers. This was criticised several times, for example in the regulations of 1686 and the marching regulations of 1691.[60]

In another mandate published in 1684 John George prompted the regimental commanders and their staff officers to take care, that the rank and file received their payment regularly through their officers. To reduce corruption the colonels of all infantry and cavalry regiments had to keep detailed muster lists of their regiments which were to be sealed and sent to the Secret War Council. Each month they had to report possible changes.[61]

The publication of the 1682 regulations was immediately followed by a flood of complaints about units which demanded more than what the regulations allowed. From the Thuringian Circle, massive protests reached the court in Dresden about the Lifeguards, those soldiers also pressed money from their quarter hosts. The interesting fact is, that most of the accused incidents happened before the 28 January – the date when the mandate was officially published – but the lawsuits were mostly not formulated before March, indicating that there was not that much unlawful behaviour of the troops after the mandate was published, but instead that subjects were simply trying to get money back from the state.[62]

While the infantry was quartered in towns, the cavalry was put into the villages and small towns of nobles. The distribution was based on the three-score tax, created in 1546 from late medieval forms of taxes. All property of the subjects was counted in tax-three scores (an accounting unit). In 1628 the worth of property in all circles was estimated at seven million thaler, but because of the losses of the Thirty Years' War it fell to five million in the 1680s. This was the basis for the distribution of horses, so in 1682 on every 1,324 tax three-scores came one horse. Another form of distribution not based on tax income but on land (*Hufe*), used from 1668 until the early 1680s, did not prove workable, but in 1684 the tax-based form was resolved by the estates.[63]

The secundogeniture duchies especially lamented the burdens of quartering. No march-through of electoral troops through Weißenfels, Merseburg or Zeitz passed without vigorous complaints being sent to Dresden (and other courts also). Dresden had its share of these conflicts, because the quartering was not always declared beforehand as it was negotiated. The municipal councils cleverly exploited this situation and wrote letters of complaint to their dukes as soon as troops were quartered. So in 1685/86 the citizens of Oelsnitz murmured about the fact that soldiers were billeted only on the poor, while the rich citizens were free of quartering.[64] This was

---

60   Mandat 1686; March-Reglement 1691.
61   Schuster/Francke, *Geschichte der Sächsischen Armee*, pp. 111–112.
62   See SächsHsta DD 11237-880.
63   Minckwitz, 'Die wirtschaftlichen Einrichtungen', pp. 314–317.
64   Thenius, *Die Anfänge des stehenden Heerwesens*, p. 23.

a clear case of double standards, because the same upper class had a high interest to keep soldiers outside the city walls (within which the wealthier part of the community lived) and billet them in the poorer outskirts. If rich citizens were free from quartering, this was not the fault of army officers and commissioners, but the city or town itself which brokered it that way. However, in the special case of Oelsnitz Duke Moritz Wilhelm of Saxe-Zeitz finally decided in 1690 that citizens free from quartering should pay a higher contribution.[65] Complaints about the high costs of the billeting of troops can be regarded as a standard procedure. However, no city had to take this burden alone. In most cases, parts of the quartered regiments were sent to other communities nearby or these had to pay a contribution to the town offering the quarters.

Especially recalcitrant was Duke Christian of Saxe-Merseburg. According to a conference protocol from 1686, Dresden prepared an appeal to the Emperor. Christian, it said, claimed to be a prince immediate to the Emperor, threatened the Elector with foreign military force and hindered the billeting of Saxon troops in his duchy.[66]

Contrary to the billeting of regiments, which gave them no permanent quarter, there were few standing garrisons in the Electorate. The biggest one was in Dresden, where there were four companies with a total of 800 men in 1680, to Alten-Dresden (western bank of the Elbe) and Neu-Dresden (eastern bank). Wittenberg had another garrison company (228 men in 1693) as had the fortresses Königstein (45 men), Sonnenstein in Pirna (48 men) and Stolpen (15 men). In 1686 the companies from Dresden were united in one garrison battalion. Since the reign of elector Christian I. each citizen of Dresden had to pay guard money (*Wachthaler*), which was given to the garrison companies, which in turn paid their quarters from it. In 1681 John George III changed the law. While the officers continued to pay for their quarters, common soldiers received it for free, but their clothing money was reduced by 12 groschen per year. This caused much trouble and protest in the capital. However in 1682 Bose wrote to the Elector, that the municipal council had lists of how much each citizen could contribute to the *Wachthaler*, suggesting, that Dresden was still willing to change the system back. Also, since the fire in 1685 there were many empty houses in Altendresden and the suburbs, which could be used as quarters. John George was willing to follow this suggestion. Because of the fire of 1685, which burned a huge part of Neu-Dresden, the garrison left the city for a while, but returned in November. On 1 March 1686 the Elector decided to recreate a permanent garrison as before 1682. The soldiers should again pay for their food and quarters and forward the bills to the war chest.[67]

While garrisons life in the bigger cities must have been quite lively, it seems to have been very boring for the more isolated fortresses, like Königstein.

---

65 *Ibid.*, p. 23.
66 *Ibid.*, p. 23.
67 Minckwitz, 'Die Besatzung zu Dresden, pp. 257–260; Thenius, *Die Anfänge des stehenden Heerwesens*, pp. 94–96.

The garrison helped itself by organising *kermesses* (country fairs), a practice which was abolished by John George III in 1684.[68]

5.6 Medical Care

The medical care system of early modern armies was probably better than its reputation suggests. Military medicine reacted quickly to the introduction of powder weapons, and already Hiernonymus' *Buch der Wund-Artzney* from 1497 or Hans von Gerdsdorff's *Feldbuch der Wundartznei* from 1517 gave detailed descriptions for the treatment of bullet wounds.

However, the daily medical work in the military was the treatment of the sick, not of the wounded. There were no hospitals for the Saxon army in peacetime. Sick soldiers were treated in their quarters or in civilian hospitals. The captains had to pay for this.[69]

In general, each Saxon regiment had a trained physician on its staff and each company a so-called *Feldscher* or barber surgeon, who learned his craft more by practical experience, than from book-learning. Barbers were often used for this position, because their basic duty was to shave the men twice a week. If they had to treat the sick, they received medicine from the regimental surgeon's medical chest, who in turn took a *Beckengeld* from the companies to buy pharmacy goods.[70]

However, the surgeon on regimental level was not introduced before 1688. For the 1683 campaign it seems that just John George's personal physician, a few hired surgeons and a special field pharmacist created a kind of special medical corps. The three regiments sent to Venice had no barber surgeons on company level, and just one on regimental level, which proved disastrous, because the troops suffered more from Mediterranean diseases than from enemy bullets. Maybe the high losses of this corps were responsible for the decision to introduce barber surgeons on a company level for the campaigns against the French in the Nine Years' War.[71] However, the troops campaigning in the east always suffered more through disaeases than those in the Rhine. Colonel von Birkholz, who marched with 1,500 men to Ofen in May 1688, reported in November, that just a third – 535 – were fit for service, 193 were in a hospital at Belgrade and a further 120 sick were still with the regiment. But the troops on the Rhine could also suffer much, which perhaps stemmed from the struggles over their provision between the Imperial and Saxon commissaries. On 21 August 1691 – three weeks before he died himself of disease – John George III wrote from his camp near Brettheim to the Secret War Council and estimated that maybe half his army was sick.[72]

---

68   SächsHsta DD 11237-210, fol. 197, instructions for the new commander Major Ulrich Graf Kinsky von Kynitz und Tettau from the 11 November 1684.
69   Thenius, *Die Anfänge des stehenden Heerwesens*, p. 126.
70   *Ibid.*, p. 126.
71   *Ibid.*, p. 127.
72   *Ibid.*, p. 130.

Field hospitals were established by the order of the commissary. They were provided with straw, strawsacks, poor quality woollen fabric and linens for the provision of the wounded. The men received bread, depending on their condition, wine, and meat three times a week. For the provision of the field hospital with firewood, candles and other necessities, the local inhabitants were responsible.[73]

5.7 Social Care

The fact that state social care is a development of the late nineteenth and early twentieth centuries does not mean that there was no social care mechanism in the early modern period. This was also true of the military. Of course, there were differences too between the mostly noble officers and the rank and file.

The majority of the officers in this time served until death. For 55 percent of the officers of 1682, death ended their service. Another 41 percent were discharged, in most cases to serve in another army. Only two percent received pensions later on, while another two percent died in battle or through duels.[74] The few who were fortunate enough to receive a pension were on average seven years older, when those who died during service – 59 years compared to 52 years – while those who left the army for another were on average 42.[75]

Invalid or sometimes retired officers always received a modest pension which guaranteed quite a good living in the evening of life. When Colonel Christoph Melchior von Neitschütz, commander of the fortress Königstein, was forced to retire in 1684 because of his advanced age, John George III granted him his full regular payment of 50 thalers per month as a pension.[76] *Generalfeldmarschall* von der Goltz, after he was relieved from command in 1683, received a guaranteed pension of 4,000 thalers per year.[77]

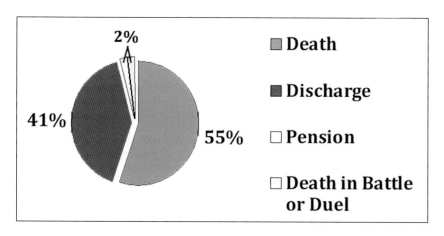

6 Reasons for end of service for Saxon officers 1682.

---

73   *Ibid.*, pp. 128–129.
74   Dethloff, *Das kursächsische Offizierskorps*, p. 335.
75   *Ibid.*, p. 342.
76   SächsHsta DD 11237-210, fol. 190, letter from the 11 November 1684.
77   SächsHsta DD 11237-209, fol. 37–38, letter of John George III. from 14 November 1683.

However, pensions and 'mercy money' (*Gnadengelder*) for widows were not paid at a fixed rate but were individual grants by the Elector who always took the financial constitution of an officer or his bereaved and their families into account. In general a widow was granted a month of her husband's full pay. After the Hungarian campaign in 1686 the widows of dead officers begged the Secret War Council for three months' payment, which was supported by the council. However, the Elector only granted one month for them. This sum in turn was retained from the payment of those who had taken over the position of the deceased, reducing the cost for this act of mercy for the Elector to nil.[78] For the first time, after von der Goltz died in 1688, his pension was granted to his sons,[79]

In some individual cases additional money was granted to the bereaved. When Colonel Caspar von Klengel died in January 1691, John George III took over the cost of the burial. However, Klengel enjoyed a very special position as educator of the princes. In 1687 the widow of a captain from regiment *Löben*, who had served on the fortress Sonnenstein, received a generous eight thalers per month, and the widow of a Lieutenant-Colonel Wolfersdorf even 30.[80]

If an officer died, he had to pay a 'dying-horse' (*Sterbepferd*). If a colonel died, his best horse with saddle and pistols or 100 ducats should be presented to the general field marshal. In the case of a staff officer, this or 50 ducats had to be presented to the colonel. From a dead captain he received this or 10 ducats in the infantry or 200 in the cavalry. Dead lieutenants or ensigns brought 20 to 30 ducats to the captains.[81]

The assets of a dead officer were held in trust by the *auditeur*, who was assisted by two officers as witnesses. Debts to the regiment were discounted, before the rest of the assers were presented to the officer's heirs. If the inheritors did not take possession, the assets would be sold by an auction.[82]

For the common soldiers there was no such system of grants and pensions. The most basic form of a 'care' system was further service. If the man was still fit for service he could stay with his company until an advancedt age. The muster roll of a company in the regiment *von der Goltz* from 23 June 1682 lists a Corporal Elias Teichstein of 71 years, who had served 31 years and seven months in various regiments.[83]

The regular social care system created by the army was the invalid penny. Of each thalers payment, three pennies were deducted for the invalid chest from which a basic provision of invalids could be granted – clothing, quarter and provisions. This measure was not introduced before 10 April 1690. According to the order of John George III it was a direct reaction to the rising casualties in recent campaigns:

---

78   Thenius, *Die Anfänge des stehenden Heerwesens*, p. 52.
79   SächsHsta DD 11237-209, fol. 49, resolution from the 22 August 1688.
80   Thenius, *Die Anfänge des stehenden Heerwesens*, p. 53.
81   *Ibid.*, p. 52.
82   *Ibid.*, p. 52.
83   *Ibid.*, p. 60.

For some time past so many of our NCOs and soldiers were wounded in the recent campaigns, that they were not able to do any further service and it must be feared, that by continuing the war, many more will lose their health, so that Christian fairness demanded, that it will be taken care for their livelihood. Because other funds for this were needed, we have decided, that of all the war etat nobody than the common soldiers, provisioner on horseman and musketeers excluded, will have three pennies deducted from each thalers which should be out in an extra chest.[84]

The expenditures for *Gnadengelder* and back pay increased during the last years of John Georges reign from 12,396 thalers in 1689 to 12,758 thalers 12 groschen in 1691 and even 14,070 thalers the year after, only falling back to 8,409 thalers in 1694.[85]

84 Quot.: HstA DD 9124/4 Remarques, Bl. 29.
85 Thenius, *Die Anfänge des stehenden Heerwesens*, p. 131.

6

Army Organisation

6.1 Army Structure

In 1684 the Elector published a regulation which ordered the ranking of the regiments within the army. Officers were always quarrelled for their prerogatives, seeing the standing of their regiment as a matter of honour. Giving a fixed hierarchy for it avoided violent outbursts about it.[1] The Guard formations were ranked senior to all others, while for the ordinary regiments the seniority of the commander was decisive. So the *Reitende Trabanten Garde* was senior within the cavalry, followed by the Lifeguards of Horse and the others. The Lifeguards on Foot were senior within the infantry, followed by the regiment of the *feldmarschall, feldmarschalllieutenant* and the others. The dragoons were regarded as separate and without rank within this hierarchy.

In most cases the army received nothing but praise from foreign princes and generals. Jan III Sobieski wrote to his wife, after seeing the Saxon infantry for the first time a few days before the battle of Vienna, 'But the guard, which arrived with him [John George III] yesterday, is very nice and in good order as is the complete army.'[2]

6.1.1 Infantry

When the army was created, each infantry regiment had eight companies. In the following years, the Lifeguards were increased to 12 companies and finally to 20 in 1692. The first company of each regiment was the colonel's, who took additional payment as the captain, as did the lieutenant-colonel for the second company and the major for the third. The others were each commanded by a captain (*Hauptmann* or *Kapitän*).[3]

The regimental staff consisted further of a regimental quartermaster, an adjutant, an auditor secretary, drummers and pipers and the provost with his aides. In 1689 a preacher, a rationmaster and a surgeon's aide

---

1   Schuster/Francke, *Geschichte der Sächsischen Armee*, p. 111.
2   Quot.: *Jan Sobieski. Briefe an die Königin. Feldzug und Entsatz von Wien 1683*, edited and commented by Joachim Zeller; (East-Berlin: Buchverlag der Morgen 1981), p. 28.
3   Thenius, *Die Anfänge des stehenden Heerwesens*, p. 75.

(*Regimentsfeldscher*), and a wagonmaster were added. This staff was called *prima plana*, because they were registered on the first page of the regimental muster list.[4]

The NCO corps of a single company consisted of three sergeants, one lance corporal (*Gefreiten-Korporal*), one *fourier*, one muster writer, one capitain d'armes, one surgeon's mate (*Feldscher*) and three corporals, together with three *tambours* (drummers). The grenadier companies had just one sergeant and no lance corporal.[5]

Additionally, a regiment had around four pipers (*Schallmey-Pfeifer*), playing French-style oboes, and two or more drummers, however, their numbers could vary.[6]

Company sizes varied: normally infantry companies were about 145 men strong, the grenadiers being weaker, starting with 64 men, but increased in size during the time.

In 1687 the distinction between 'musketeers' and 'pikemen' was given up, after the infantry was completely armed with muskets. The ordinary soldiers were now called *Gemeine* (meaning ordinary or common soldier) and *Grenadier*.[7]

Generalfeldmarschall von der Goltz in November 1682 asked for the establishment of a company of grenadiers, which was raised in the next spring under the command of Captain Heinrich von Bose at a strength of 103 men. The grenadiers immediately received an elite status and would be formed of veteran soldiers.[8]

Grenadiers were a French innovation and used hand grenades in battle. Contrary to later times, they were used as a kind of light infantry in battle and would advance in front of the main line and throw their deadly missiles at officers and gun crews.[9]

The grenadiers immediately enjoyed a reputation as the elite of the army. An undated 'project' for the creation of a grenadier company (probably from 1682), states that 'the actions, for which the granatiers were needed, are always the spirited and most dangerous.'[10] Because of this the company officers would be allowed to pick the most able men from other units, who received better payment.[11]

In 1687 more companies were raised, and officially one attached to each regiment of infantry. However, this was an administrative organisation, and tactically they were assembled into one battalion.

---

4   *Ibid.*, pp. 75–76.
5   *Ibid.*, p. 76.
6   Regarding military music, see Konrad Neefe, 'Die Entwicklung der kur- und königl. sächsischen Infanteriemusik. Von den ältesten Zeiten bis Ende des 18. Jahrhunderts', in: *NASG* 18 (1897), pp. 109–125, here pp. 110–112. However, apart from the pipers littleinformation could be obtained for the 1680s from this article.
7   Schuster/Francke, *Geschichte der Sächsischen Armee*, p. 112.
8   SächsHsta DD 11237-887, without fol, signed „Project".
9   Vgl.: Bauer, 'Organisation und Struktur', S. 226; Thenius, *Die Anfänge des stehenden Heerwesens*, p. 73.
10 Quot.: SächsHsta DD 11237-887, without fol.
11 *Ibid.*

6.1.2 Cavalry

A Saxon cavalry regiment always consisted of six companies of about 100 horse, being reduced in 1690 to 75. The regimental staff was similar to the infantry, but instead of tambours they had kettle drum players. A company staff consisted of a captain (*Rittmeister*), *Lieutnant*, *Kornet*, *Wachtmeister*, *Fourier*, three corporals, two buglers, one muster writer, one surgeon's mate, a colour smith (*Fahnenschmied*), a saddler and a cuirass maker (*Plattner*). A full-size company had 86 troopers.[12]

The dragoon regiments were of similar size, but had a bigger band with 24 pipers and six *tambours* and – contrary to the cuirassiers – a captain d'armes, but two horsemen less.[13] Dragoons were still considered as mounted infantry. This can also be seen by the use of the German term *Reiter* (horsemen or trooper), which was only used for cuirassiers, while the term 'dragoon' itself demonstrated a separation.

6.1.3 Artillery

The Saxon artillery enjoyed a good reputation but had the most traditional organisation, more like a civilian guild. Gunnery was still a craft and everybody who wanted to join this branch had to take an examination at the Main Arsenal in Dresden first. Gunners were not organised in companies before the reign of John George's son August – with the exception of a short-lived free company of gunners in 1688 – and fixed batteries not before the end of the eighteenth century. For a campaign, individual guns and gunners were assigned to army corps or regiments. Typically 16-pounder howitzers, 8-pounder field guns and 3- and 6-pounder regimental guns were used, drawn by teams of two, six or eight horses.[14]

Responsible for the artillery lay with Colonel Wolff Caspar von Klengel, who received a monthly salary of 150 thaler.[15] While there was no fixed organisation for the artillery, this branch at least had a kind of administrative and logistical centre in form of the Main Arsenal in Dresden. Here, gunners and various kinds of craftsmen were employed, for example specialised powder makers, who worked at a powder mill outside the city walls.[16]

The artillery as a branch might not have been very attractive to noble officers, but that does not mean that it was completely unattractive to the high nobility. Artillery was still a sport for kings. This can be seen in the fact that in 1680 the 10-year-old prince Friedrich August was introduced to the art of gunnery through Colonel von Klengel and took a successful examination in the same year.[17]

Even in the late seventeenth century the art of the gunner was similar to that of a fireworker, and the artillery used a wide range of ammunition as can

---

12 Thenius, *Die Anfänge des stehenden Heerwesens*, p. 76.
13 *Ibid.*, p. 77.
14 *Ibid.*, p. 77.
15 SächsHsta DD 11237-215, fol. 7.
16 See the commission of Claus Borzigk from 1 June 1683, SächsHsta DD 11237-213, without fol.
17 A. von Kretzschmar, *Die Geschichte der kurfürstlich und königlich sächsischen Feldartillerie von 1620–1820* (Berlin: without company 1876), p. 140.

be seen from a letter of John George III to Colonel Klengel. When he visited Venice in 1685 the Elector was able to inspect the Venetian arsenal, but he showed himself very disappointed about the quality of the Venetian gunners:

> I have seen their samples and their art, they are almost worse than the Strasburgers have been, it disappointed me, no real mortars, no carcasses, no grenades with real fire, no fireballs well bounded, they know of no burning stones and no fireball is not bought. They store and sweep in their mortars even more severely than the Strasburger and yet do not throw as far; it was luck, that it did not cause any damage, because the powder was too weak, otherwise it could not have been carried out like this, while 100 ladies and cavaliers were standing nearby without the common, the balls[18] were always falling 20 or 30 paces in front or behind us.[19]

This letter implies that the Saxon artillery not only used balls, canister and grenades or bombs but a wide range of chemical projectiles. It also testifies in impressive manner, that the art of gunnery was not yet an established international science, but more of an old-fashioned craft, where quality and accuracy depended largely on the skills of the gunner as producer of ammunition.

Engineers were assigned to the artillery. There was no *état* for them and they were probably hired for single campaigns. We know of one engineer officer on the Vienna campaign of 1683 and seven during the war with France. They were responsible for planning fieldworks or bridges, and their workers were hired on the spot. For example when a bridge was built at Weißenau in the south of Mainz, carpenters were hired for four weeks, as was a 'bridge captain', three 'bridge corporals', four carpenters for repairs and 24 aids, showing once more, that military 'outsourcing' was already a common practice of this time.[20]

6.2 Uniforms and Equipment

Unfortunately, there is little information about uniform detail. We have no coloured period images and most contemporary documents only give information about the quantities of certain items which were ordered, and none about their appearance.[21] The uniforms were ordered by the individual colonels who were also responsible for their design. The colonel created a muster and ordered the lieutenant-colonel or major to buy fabric, which was either finished by tailors within the regiment or within communal guilds. In

---

18   The Elector here uses two terms, which can both be translated with balls, *Kugeln* meaning cannonballs, and *Ballen*, meaning fireballs.
19   Quot.: Kretzschmar, *Feldartillerie*, p. 141.
20   Thenius, *Die Anfänge des stehenden Heerwesens*, p. 79.
21   The standard work for uniform enthusiasts still is: Wolfgang Friedrich, *Die Uniformen der kurfürstlich-sächsischen Armee, Vol. 1 1683–1763* (Dresden: Selbstverlag des Arbeitskreises Sächsische Militärgeschichte e.V. 1997).

11 Illustration of Gabriel Tschimmer, *Die Durchlauchtigste Zusammenkunft*, showing the *Underguardia*, the communal guard of Dresden in 1678. It is one of the few period images representing Saxon military and flags, however, not a regular army formation. This illustration shows in the background a formation of the Underguardia on the New Market.

general, each unit should receive new uniforms every three years – a long time, especially when on campaign.[22]

The infantry regiments received grey coats, except for the Lifeguards who wore a much more impressive red. It was not before the reign of John George's second son Augustus the Strong that the whole army received red uniforms. In the 1680s the regiments were distinguished from each other by the colour of their *doublure*. This term was used for collars and turnbacks, which were the colour of the lining fabric. The metal of the buttons (brass or tin) was also used to this end.[23]

The gunners of the artillery received blue-greyish tunics with green turnbacks and vests. The trousers were of leather, the leather gear of a natural colour. The hat cords were black-yellow, possibly as a reference to the colours of the city of Dresden. The gunners were stationed in the capital and had to fulfil various representative tasks there.[24]

Before the campaign of 1691 the gunners received new uniforms and were issued grey coats lined with red boy. Collars and turnbacks were also red.[25]

---

22 Thenius, *Die Anfänge des stehenden Heerwesens*, pp. 82–83; Friedrich, *Die Uniformen*, p. 4.
23 Friedrich, *Die Uniformen*, p. 4.
24 *Ibid.*, p. 4.
25 Schuster/Francke, *Geschichte der Sächsischen Armee*, pp. 118–119.

The cavalry already had uniform dress by 1673. It was also planned to introduce distinguishing colours for the different regiments, but this never happened. Only the colours, sash and trumpet flags had these. The cuirassiers wore a buff leather coat and a cuirass with front and back part above it. In 1680 helmets were still common showing an eastern European influence (*Zischägge*). Trousers were of buff leather also or of thick red woollen fabric, tucked into heavy riding boots. Trumpeters had no cuirass and no helmet but instead wore a hat.[26] The Lifeguard of Horse had had red uniforms since their creation. These were decorated in the colours of the dynasty, blue and gold.[27]

The grenadiers had blue caps and stockings. After the grenadier battalion was split up and the individual companies given to the ordinary infantry regiments, a change of uniform was ordered too. The men now should get red coats with blue collars and facings. Until these new coats were issued, the old grey ones would be updated and blue collars and facings attached to them. The men received black cartridge boxes with yellow slings for four grenades and a dozen cartridges.[28] According to a bill from 1683 the grenadiers also received raincoats (*Regenröcke*), for 1 thaler 6 groschen each. The uniform cost 10 thaler, the cap 2.[29]

According to a bill from the Lifeguards of Foot, they too received raincoats (worth 3 Thaler), while their hats just cost 14 groschen.[30] According to bills from the Lifeguards of Foot from 1684, the men received canteens and packs

12 This is probably the only surviving example of a Saxon infantry flag of John George III's period. It was captured by the Swedish army at the battle of Fraustadt in 1706, but differs in style from the typical flags of Frederick August I's period and also from the Thirty Years' War period, so it was probably made between 1650 and 1694. (Armémuseum Stockholm, creative commons license CC BY <https://creativecommons.org/licenses/by/4.0/deed.en>; grayscaled)

26 Friedrich, *Die Uniformen*, p. 4.
27 *Ibid.*, p. 4.
28 Schuster/Francke, *Geschichte der Sächsischen Armee*, p. 112.
29 SächsHsta DD 11237-209, fol. 223.
30 SächsHsta DD 11237-9130/19, without fol.

(*Ranzen*), but we do not know what they looked like. Another bill presented the costs for both at 17 groschen.[31]

The militia was equipped with grey coats with red turnbacks and tin buttons, grey trousers and black hats. Because the equipment was provided by the communities themselves, the look of the men varied greatly.[32]

6.3 Weapons

Weapons were provided by the Elector. Each company received its muskets from the Main Arsenal in Dresden. Additionally company commanders received four thalers monthly (*Gewehrgelder*) to replace broken or lost muskets. However, this practice was expensive and did not work. In general broken guns were replaced or paid for by the Elector.[33]

The Saxon infantry received matchlock muskets and while the infantry was originally organised as pikeneers and musketeers, all pikes were handed over to the arsenal in Dresden in 1683 and the men completely armed with muskets.

In 1688 the first flintlock muskets were offered to the infantry. However, the army seemed to have been suspicious of the new weapon system and furnished the guns with a combined lock of flint and match. According to a bill from 1683, the grenadiers already had flintlocks, costing 2.5 thalers each.[34]

The cartridge boxes of the infantry would contain 24 cartridges, and the smaller grenadier boxes, worn on the belt in front of the body, three iron grenades.[35]

Infantrymen also had sidearms. However, the first standard model was not made for Saxon troops before 1700, so the styles in John George's area varied. It was also not unusual to rework older models, which were collected im large numbers in the arsenal in Dresden, so often old blades were fitted with a new handle. The bayonets used were still plug-style; the Military History Museum in Dresden has a considerable collection of these bayonets in various styles. The cavalry – cuirassiers and dragoons alike – used broadswords with a long blade and brass Degen basket. Cuirassiers also received pistols, but no specific type can be attributed to this period.

6.4 The Militia

As was shown in the first chapter, Saxony during the seventeenth century never found a satisfying organisation for its militia. However, also after the creation of a standing army John George did not want to relinquish of this additional military potential. In 1681, 1682 and 1683 the Elector repeatedly

31 SächsHsta DD 11237-9130/19, without fol.
32 Thenius, *Die Anfänge des stehenden Heerwesens*, p. 63.
33 *Ibid.*, p. 84.
34 SächsHsta DD 11237-209, fol. 223.
35 Thenius, *Die Anfänge des stehenden Heerwesens*, p. 81.

13, 14 Saxon matchlock musket of the 1680s. (Armémuseum Stockholm)

15, 16 Older Saxon matchlock musket, probably of the 1660s. Guns like these were probably only issued to the militia.
(Armémuseum Stockholm)

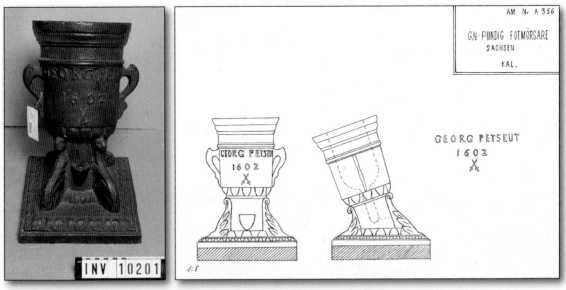

17, 18 A lot of older guns were used by the Saxon army. During the Great Northern War (1700–1721), Swedish troops captured numerous Saxon guns. This mortar of the period of Elector Christian II, cast in 1602, was taken after the surrender of Fort Augustusburg/Dünamünde in 1701, which indicates that it could also have been used in the age of John George III, for example during the sieges of the Rhine campaigns. (Armémuseum Stockholm)

19, 20, 21, 22, 23 This heavy 24-pounder was cast in the reign of John George III (cast in 1686) and also taken by the Swedes at Augustusburg. It was too heavy for field use and was only used for sieges or on fortresses. (Armeemuseum Stockholm)

INV 10216

INV 10216

24, 25 Six-pounders like this one were the heaviest pieces used in the field. This gun, cast in 1685, was also captured at Dünemünde. (Armeemuseum Stockholm)

asked the estates to raise the *defensioner* but received nothing but complaints, so they remained suspended. When in 1683 John George left Saxony with nearly the complete new army to fight the Turks in front of Vienna, the militia was put in readiness. A real call to arms was avoided because of the additional costs this would create, 'to the conservation of the country, whose complete ruin threatened.'[36]

In 1684 John George prepared another proposal for a reorganisation of the militia which once more was turned down by the estates. They argued convincingly that a militia system had never been very effective but only expansive and that it seemed doubtful even to try a reorganisation, now that a formidable standing army was established. John George accepted these arguments. To demonstrate that the system was still not officially disbanded, he published patents from time to time, putting the companies of horse and foot in readiness. He asked for 1,500 men and another 1,500 to be held in reserve. Militiamen should be offered tax incentives. However, because there

---

36   Quot.: Friesen, 'Das "Defensionswesen"', p. 223.

never was a serious threat from a foreign power to the Electorate itself, there was no need to call them to arms.[37]

In 1688 the Elector once more called up the militia, after the army left the country. The men would be provided with new cartridge boxes for two thalers each.[38]

Not necessarily as a real reform, but rather to increase the attractiveness of the service, on 31 May 1689 John George granted the men a payment of two groschen a day and ordered, that their neighbours should cultivate their fields in times of service, if they were not bigger than half a *Hufe*.[39] In the same year it was decided to levy militiaman by lot.[40] A new regulation for the militia demanded that the men were given muskets of the same calibre.[41]

The threat of invasion became real in 1706, when during the Great Northern War and the crushing defeat of a regular Saxon army at the field of Fraustadt, the Swedish army under Charles XII invaded Saxony, meeting no resistance at all. Because of this Augustus the Strong declared, on 4 May 1708, that 'the old defence system, because it is as expensive as the same number of hired troops and and yet is of no use – one can not rely on old and infirm men – is now completely disbanded in all areas.'[42] Instead of this, he created a completely new system. Each circle or province now had to provide its own militia regiment of three battalions with four companies each. Eight such regiments were created and called to arms from time to time later in the Great Northern War. They proved very effective.

Apart from militia systems, citizens of fortified towns (also those of the majority of towns which only had outdated medieval fortifications) were responsible for defending them in time of siege. When the majority of the army left Saxony in 1688 to fight the French, John George III instructed the municipal councils of the towns Freyburg, Zwickau and Chemnitz, 'that the citizens be provided with guns and will be drilled diligently and also mustered.'[43]

6.5 Tactics

The tactical organisation in 1682 established a six-rank formation with two-thirds of musketeers and one third of pikemen. Each file consisted of five common soldiers and one *Gefreiter*, a kind of private first class, who was not considered as an NCO.[44] This was an organisation quite typical of western European armies of the time, combining the firepower of the musketeers with

---

37 *Ibid.*, pp. 223–224.
38 SächsHsta DD 11237-1059, without fol, instruction of John George III, 27 November 1688.
39 Thenius, *Die Anfänge des stehenden Heerwesens*, p. 63.
40 Dietzel, 'Zur Militärverfassung', p. 434.
41 SächsHsta DD 11237-463, fol. 124.
42 Quot.: Alexander Querengässer, 'Von der Landesdefension zu den Kreisregimentern. Das kursächsische Milizwesen im Großen Nordischen Krieg 1700 bis 1716', in: *Zeitschrift für Heereskunde* 459 (2016), pp. 2–8.
43 Quot.: SächsHsta DD 11237-1059, without fol. Instructions of the Elector from 27 November 1688.
44 Schuster/Francke, *Geschichte der Sächsischen Armee*, p. 98.

defensive stability provided by the pike. However already by the time of their first campaign the infantry regiments had abandoned the pike and armed all men with muskets and a so called *Schweinsfeder* (swinefeather), a short pike of five or six feet, which could be put into a wooden bar to form *cheveaux-de-frise*, behind which the musketeers could take cover. This displacement of musketeers had already proved to be very effective against the Ottomans, who used masses of light cavalry and infantry formations which in turn were also more used to defensive than offensive tactics. At the battle of Vienna the Saxon infantry proved to be very effective in advance. After the regimental pieces had fired, the battalions advanced 30 to 40 pieces and gave their own volley. After the cannons had been reloaded, they were brought forward and the game repeated itself.[45]

The cavalry preferred firepower to cold steel, using the slow 'caracole'. The dragoons were not yet a full cavalry force, but more of a mounted infantry. At Vienna they supported infantry attacks dismounted, and also gave flank protection in a kind of light order.

The role of the grenadiers is particularly interesting. While during the late 1680s the companies of the regiments would be combined into one battalion during campaign, *Generalfeldmarschall* von Schöning's drill regulations called for the use of grenadiers in small groups in front of the infantry line. Here they would work more as a kind of light infantry, disrupting the formation of the enemy. Also the instructions explicitly mentioned that they should go for officers or gunners, a tactic which is nowadays more connected with the French army during the Revolution, but was everything but uncommon in the seventeenth century.

During the mobilisation for the campaign in 1683 the structure of the army changed slightly: John George determined that the six companies of a cavalry regiment in battle should form three squadrons.[46] Also the arrangement of the infantry in squadrons was given up. Instead, two battalions of four companies each per regiment were now created.[47]

In 1685 the army assembled for the first time for a so-called exercise camp (*Exerzierlager*) near Torgau. On 22 June all regiments were assembled near the city and held individual drill and joint manoeuvres. However, few details are known about the camp.[48]

In 1687 a new manual was introduced for the complete army by the order of the Elector. This would guarantee, that all regiments used the same kind of drill. Heretofore different manuals were used by the colonels. Now a kind of seminary was established in Dresden which had to be attended by one adjutant per regiment and an NCO from each company. Here they were taught from the new manual by a Captain Alberti.[49] While this was a very sensible measure, methods of recruitment complicated its observance. Particularly when new regiments were hired by foreign princes or were

45 Hassel/Vitzthum von Eckstädt, *Zur Geschichte des Türkenkrieges*, pp. 158–159.
46 Schuster/Francke, *Geschichte der Sächsischen Armee*, pp. 102–103.
47 *Ibid.*, pp. 102–103.
48 *Ibid.*, p. 112.
49 *Ibid.*, p. 11; Bauer, 'Organisation und Struktur', S. 226.

raised from scratch, it could not be guaranteed that they used the mandatory drill. This became an even more serious problem, when the number of units increased during the reign of John George's son Augustus the Strong. In 1701 the acting *feldmarschall* of the army, Adam Heinrich von Steinau, advised the Elector-king to hold a general exercise camp to unify the drill of the troops. According to the 1687 manual a company was broken up for the march into three platoons (*Züge*) with four or six ranks.

In general it can be said that while the Saxon army developed its own drill regulations, these did not differ much from those of other western and central European armies of this time. Even after the infantry was completely armed with muskets, it lacked the combination of firepower and cold steel provided by the bayonet musket of the eighteenth century, because the pikemen were only replaced by *chevaux-de-frise*, diminishing every 'revolutionary' effect one might attribute to it. As noted above, the cavalry favoured guns to blades. This proved to be effective against the Ottoman troops and was no disadvantage against the French, who used the same tactics, but would prove fatal against the Swedes in the Great Northern War, whose cavalry attacked with drawn swords. The fact that gunnery was more of a craft than a military profession was true throughout Europe, even if it might be admitted, that this craft was highly developed in Saxony.

6.6 Fortresses

Fortresses played only a minor role for Saxon war history in this time and even their economic role during the reign was negligible, because not much money was spent for the preservation or expansion of existing fortresses.

However, fortresses and fortified places were not only important for the defence of the country, but functioned as regional arsenals. Just a handful of such places existed in Saxony; however, they could be separated into three categories: fortified residences, border guard grounds and protections for river crossings (on the Elbe).[50]

The most important fortress of the country was the city of Dresden itself. The city was once the first modern fortress in the trace 'Italienne' style north of the Alps and east of the Rhine. Erected by Elector Maurice in the middle of the sixteenth century it was modernised through Elector Christian I (*r.* 1590–1591) and John George I during the Thirty Years' War. The city was the capital, and because of the stone bridges over the Elbe was a very important river crossing. The *Hauptzeughaus* (Main Arsenal) was one of the biggest arsenals in Europe, storing modern and old weapons and war booty. The several *Landzeughäuser* (land arsenals) mostly stored older weapons which in times of war would be handed to the militia.[51]

---

50 Manfred Lachmann, *Gliederung und Garnisonen der sächsischen Armee vom Aufkommen des stehenden Heeres bis zum Ende der Monarchie* (Atlas zur Geschichte und Landeskunde von Sachsen, Beiheft zur Karte D III 3) (Leipzig – Dresden: Verlag der Sächsischen Akademie der Wissenschaften zu Leipzig und Landesvermessungsamt Sachsen 2008), S. 8–9.

51 *Ibid.*, pp. 8–9.

Table 10 Fortresses and fortified places in Saxony[52]

Name	Type	Category			Arsenal
		Residence	**Border Guard**	**River Crossing**	
Dresden	Fortress	X		X (Elbe)	Main Arsenal
Königstein	Fortress		X	X (Elbe)	Land Arsenal
Wittenberg	Fortress	(former Residence)	X	X (Elbe)	Land Arsenal
Leipzig	Fortified City and Fortress (Pleißen-burg)				Land Arsenal
Torgau	Fortress	Former Residence		X (Elbe)	Land Arsenal
Freiberg	Fortified City				
Stolpen	Fortress				Land Arsenal
Zwickau	Fortified City				Land Arsenal
Heldrungen	Fort		X		Land Arsenal
Freyburg an der Unstrut	Fortified City				Land Arsenal

26 A reconstructed birdseye view of the city of Chemnitz about 1750. The medieval fortification of the town can still be seen. (K. Haustein, 1907)

52 Lachmann, *Gliederung und Garnisonen der sächsischen Armee*, p. 9.

27 A late sixteenth century view of Görlitz, a major town in Lusatia, also protected by medieval fortifications of the fifteenth century. (Colourised engraving by Georgius Bruin and Frans Hogenberg, from *De Praecipuis, Totius Universi Urbibus, Liber Secundus*, Cologne 1575)

28 The capital, Dresden, was the best-fortified place in the Electorate. The picture shows Altendresden (confusingly nowadays called 'Neustadt' on the eastern bank of the Elbe river), before it was destroyed in a fire in 1685. (From Bruno Krause, *Die geschichtliche Entwickelung der... Residenzstadt Dresden... Mit... Illustrationen, etc.*, Dresden 1893)

29 Dresden in 1687. The stone bridge origins probably from the twelfth century and gives strategic importance to the city. (From: C. Schneider: *Ausführliche und grundrichtige Beschreibung des ganzen Elb-Stroms.* Nürnberg 1687)

Dresden had had a permanent garrison since 1587 which was reformed several times through the years. John George III disbanded these troops in 1682 and used them to fill up the newly created regiments. The capital now became the garrison of the Lifeguards of Foot.[53]

However, in times of war the many towns with outdated medieval walls were also instructed to improve their fortifications. So in November 1688 the Elector wrote to the towns of Freiburg, Zwickau and Chemnitz, that:

30 Apart from Dresden, the fortress of Senfternberg in Lower Lusatia was the only reliable modern fortification with bastions. (Photo: Andreas Praefcke, public domain)

> The cities, their gates and bridges, also where else it might be essential, will be well provided with tollgates, also that the portcullis, if existing, will be put into a good condition, the cities will have ditches excavated and cleared, also that the outer wards and towers will be put in a serviceable condition for defence, and all open places will be provided with palisades.[54]

Instructions like this were very often read by the municipal councils and afterwards ignored. In this case, Zwickau answered on 3 December, that the citizen guard was drilling, and that much effort was put into the improvement of the fortifications, for which workers were hired and also citizens delegated. However, wood for palisades was difficult to get and there had been no volunteers for clearing the ditches.[55] Apart from these smaller problems, it is quite astonishing that Zwickau followed the order. The council of Leipzig also claimed to have started some work but made the hard weather responsible for it not being able to improve the walls, and said the fortifications in

---

53   Minckwitz, 'Die Besatzung zu Dresden', p. 254.
54   Quot.: SächsHsta DD 11237-1059, without fol, instructions of John George III from 27 November 1688.
55   *Ibid*, without fol, letter from 3 December 1688.

general had been in a very sad condition. Later they demanded financial help to improve them.[56] Chemnitz rejected the order immediately, arguing that it only received 200 of the guaranteed 1,000 thalers the Elector had promised to pay and that the city had already spent many thousands in recent years for the improvement of the fortifications. They promised to continue the works but begged for the other 800 thaler.[57]

6.7 Logistics

For a long time early modern military and state development was measured by the state of military state control achieved in the late nineteenth and early twentieth century. The more or less absolute state monopoly of violence and completely state-administered military system became an ideal and a target to which the development of the early modern period aimed at. Because of this teleological approach it is no wonder that historians spoke of the armies of the late seventeenth century as 'at a standstill' or 'stood still, halfway through the process of being taken over by the government.' However in the 30 years since the end of the Cold War the attitude of modern states toward a state-controlled military has changed. The Western world saw considerable military outsourcing, manifested in the name 'Blackwater', a mercenary agency hiring soldiers to the USA. But absolute control of the state over the military, even during the zenith of state control in the autocratic 'total' states of the early twentieth century, is a fiction. Even National Socialist Germany ordered its weapons for the *Wehrmacht* from private corporations such as Krupp, Porsche, Messerschmidt and Junkers. Today, all western states have outsourced many parts of their military apparatus, from the construction of weapon systems (from handguns to aircraft carriers), logistics (from toilets and vehicles to food) to their monopoly of violence in battle (Blackwater) or border control (Frontex as a European example). Considering all this, the questions seems more than legitimate, that if the modern state which once enjoyed the ideal of more or less absolute control over its military system, started to outsource huge parts of this control to private contractors, who delivered good quality for much lower prices, why should the early modern state, lacking the financial capacities of its successor, ever have thought about 'insourcing' them?[58]

For transport the army relied on two feudal relics. The most important one was the army wagon system (*Heerwagenverordnung*), according to which towns and cities had to provide wagons for the campaign; the other was simple feudal service. The raising of the *Heerwagen* was reorganised several times, lastly in 1620. According to this organisation, the *Amt* Dresden for example had to provide 12½ wagons, 124 trabants and 25 teamsters.[59] All in

---

56 *Ibid*, without fol, letter from 10 November 1688, 15 December 1688.
57 *Ibid*., without fol., letter from the 11 January 1689.
58 A good introduction to this wide-ranging topic is David Parrott, *The Business of War. Military Enterprise and Military Revolution in Early Modern Europe* (Cambridge: Cambridge University Press 2012).
59 SächsHsta DD 11237-10817/14, fol. 11–16.

all – according to a list from 1588, which was still used in the seventeenth century – the various *Ämter* in Saxony had to send 486 wagons, 1,964 horses, 829 teamsters and 4,949 trabants for the army.[60] While the trabants as a form of peasant infantry were no longer of any use, the wagons were vital for the army transport system.

Feudal services could only be used within the electorate over a small local area. The mandate of 1682 made it clear that 'No wagon service will be given without payment in cash but instead for each wagon no matter if drawn by 4, 3 or 3 horses, 12 groschen be paid and not taken further than to the next quarter and sent back unharmed.'[61] So for additional baggage new wagons had to be required from quarter to quarter, while it is not clear how this was handled outside the Electorate. However, this seems to have been insufficient. The marching regulations of 1691 complained that officers demanded too many additional wagons from local communities and kept them longer than allowed. It once more fixed the number of wagons per company at two for cavalry and three for infantry regiments, otherwise 12 horses or 18 oxen with the same number for the regimental staff.[62]

However, these were for the army's baggage trains. The wagons used by the individual companies were bought. For example in February 1684

31 Period engraving of a wagon train. Logistics were essential to warmaking in every period, but was a weakness of the Saxon army in this time, due to a lack of experience and repeated attempts to make the Emperor responsible for it. (Engraving by Jan van Huchtenburg (1657–1733), after Adam Frans van der Meulen (1632–1690))

---

60   See the full record SächsHsta DD 11237-2308.
61   Quot.: Mandat über die Neuordnung des Militärwesens im Kurfürstentum Sachsen, January 1682.
62   March-Reglement 1691.

Lieutenant-Colonel Hans Rudolph von Schönfeld complained, that he had not yet received the 133 thalers needed to buy and equip a baggage wagon.[63] For the 1683 Vienna campaign each regimental staff and company were assigned thee wagons.[64]

In the field each company was accompanied by one or two *vivandieres*, who carried or bought additional food and drinks. They had their own contracts with the colonels, who took care that the *vivandieres* did not demand too high prices. In peacetime, *vivandieres* were not allowed.[65]

The regulations of 1691 set out daily marching distances of two miles to three and a half miles (one Saxon mile according to the Codex Augusteus of 1722 was 9,062 metres or 9,910 yards). Under normal circumstances a unit should march three days and then receive a day of rest, a under special circumstances the third day could be used.[66]

The same regulations fixed the portions (for men) and rations (for beasts). Soldiers should receive two pounds of bread, one and a half *Maaß* (two litres) of the local beer or one of wine. Horses received eight pounds of hay and straw.[67]

· 32 Soldiers and vivandieres in camp. While the number of camp followers in the later part of the seventeenth century was probably smaller than during the Thirty Years' War – when their numbers often have been two or three times that of the field army – they would still have been considerable. (Engraving by Jan van Huchtenburg (1657–1733))

63   SächsHsta DD 11237-9130/19, without fol.
64   Hassel / Vitzthum von Eckstädt, *Zur Geschichte des Türkenkrieges*, p. 110.
65   Thenius, *Die Anfänge des stehenden Heerwesens*, p. 102.
66   March-Reglement 1691.
67   March-Reglement 1691.

7

From Guns to Tents: The Army and the Economy

The Saxon army was able to cover a huge part of its own demand for muskets from its own manufacturers. The small town of Suhl in the middle of the Thuringian forest was known throughout Europe for the fine quality of its guns. The town belonged to the county of Hennegau which in turn was part of the Duchy of Saxe-Zeitz. Another, much smaller, centre for gun production was Olbernhau in the Erzgebirge. Here muskets and pistols were manufactured by a few specialised craftsmen, but organised manufacture was not set up before the reign of August the Strong.

Arms were often bought by or for individual regiments. In January 1686 a gunsmith called Lorenz provided 453 bayonets and in the following march 500 matchlock muskets were provided for the regiment *Saxe-Weißenfels*.[1]

For the supply with ammunition, several powder mills existed in Saxony. One of the oldest was located outside Dresden on the small riverlet Weißeritz. It was established by an electoral degree in 1576. On 29 July 1689 the mill exploded because of an accident but was soon re-established.[2] Saxony produced a large amount of powder in this time and even exported some. In the late 1680s Jan III Sobieski bought powder and ammunition for his troops in Dresden.[3] The arsenal here also had an own foundry, where guns could be cast.

We only have a little information about the production of uniforms. However, considering the fact that uniform manufacture was not established before the reign of August the Strong, we can assume that uniforms during John George's reign were made completely by local craftsman in communal guilds, as this was a common practice right into the eighteenth century. Uniforms could either be ordered by merchants, who in turn had them made in the guilds, or the regimental commanders bought fabric separately and handed it over to local tailors.

---

1   Schuster/Francke, *Geschichte der Sächsischen Armee*, p. 112.
2   *Ibid.*, p. 117.
3   Kretzschmar, *Feldartillerie*, p. 5.

33 The arsenal in Dresden was not just a storehouse, but also a production centre, where guns were cast and bladed weapons produced. (From Bruno Krause, *Die geschichtliche Entwickelung der... Residenzstadt Dresden... Mit... Illustrationen, etc.*, Dresden 1893)

8

The Army on Campaign

8.1 Baptism of Fire: The Battle of Vienna, 1683

In 1664 Austria signed a peace treaty limited to 20 years with the Ottoman Empire. By 1682 negotiations were taken up to extend it, but the Austrian diplomats failed in the attempt to come to a new agreement with the Turks. War was in the air. On 26 January 1683 Austria signed a defensive alliance with Bavaria, and in March news reached the court in Vienna that a huge 168,000 men strong Turkish army under the Pope was able to form a new Holy Alliance with King Jan III Sobieski of Poland.[1]

In spring the Ottoman army started its march up the Danube. The Habsburg forces under Charles of Lorraine were too weak to resist them and started an orderly retreat. On 11 July Kara Mustafa reached Vienna. The first siege in 1529 being well remembered, the capital and residence of the Austrian Habsburgs was heavily fortified following modern criteria. The garrison consisted of 15,000 men, including communal guards. On the other hand the Ottomans were masters of siege warfare and their army was accompanied by French engineers.

It was his worry about the unabated aggression of France which prompted John George III to join an association of southern and western German princes, and ensure they maintained a permanent army of 10,000 men. Additionally the Elector signed an alliance with the Emperor, to whom he promised the provision of 4,700 soldiers for the defence of the Habsburg hereditary lands. The ink on the document was barely dry, when on 21 June

---

1   A remarkably well-written account of the Turkish Wars and the Saxon involvement can be found in: Holger Schuckelt, *Die Türckische Cammer. Sammlung orientalischer Kunst in der kurfürstlich-sächsischen Rüstkammer Dresden* (Dresden: Sandstein Verlag 2010), pp. 156–224. This is mostly based on an older essay of the same author: Holger Schuckelt, 'Die Rolle Sachsens in den Türkenkriegen des 16. und 17. Jahrhunderts', in: *Im Lichte des Halbmonds. Das Abendland und der türkische Orient. Ausstellungskatalog* (Dresden: Sandstein Verlag 1995), pp. 170–177. Older: Hassel/Vitzthum von Eckstädt, *Zur Geschichte des Türkenkrieges*, pp. 58–60.

1683 the Imperial ambassador Count Lamboy reached Dresden and asked for the help of Saxony in support of the pressed Vienna.[2]

John George III was quickly ready to follow this call and march out with his whole army. Of cause he did not act just out of pure Christian charity. The Elector immediately sent the Duke of Saxe-Lauenburg to Passau and wrote to Secret War Council member von Schott in Ratisbon to negotiate the details of a new contract. John George demanded that his troops would be supplied in the Habsburg hereditary lands and also that he would be given overall command of all German troops. But the last point was neither in the interest of the Elector of Bavaria –who also joined the relieving army with a comparable force – nor Charles of Lorraine, the Imperial commander. The Emperor could not be moved to more than vague and imprecise evidences of favour. In the end, the contact with Saxony was worse compared to those with Bavaria and Brunswick-Lüneburg, both of which were granted substantial financial compensation. Saxony received nothing, not least because John George III relied on the Imperial war constitution and made no separate demands.[3]

Because of this the departure of the Saxon troops was delayed. But sluggish negotiations with the Emperor had not been the only reasons. The high costs for mobilisation also slowed things down. The artillery alone needed 47,291 thalers to procure horses, wagons, teamsters and piece servants for the artillery, but only 18,000 could be provided. Because of this, the field artillery had to be reduced from 24 to 16 pieces. During the absence of nearly the complete army, the militia had to be called to arms to support the few regular companies left behind to garrison the fortresses.[4]

Because the negotiations in Passau still produced no results, the Saxon estates pressed the Elector to at least not join the campaign personally, if he was not willing to abandon it completely. But a warlike nature such as John George's hoped for new military glory and – at least so it seems in the light of the events to come – might still speculate for more than the command of his own troops. Beneath *Feldmarschal* von der Goltz, *Feldmarschallieutnants* Flemming and Duke Christian of Saxe-Weißenfels, and *Generalwachtmeister* von Neitschütz, a big part of his court followed him, all in all 337 persons with 373 horses. During his absence, von Haugwitz of the Secret War Council led the civilian administration.[5]

The electoral army was assembled between July 25 and 27 near Dresden between the old Ziegelscheune and the fir grove of Blasewitz.[6] It consisted of six cavalry and six infantry regiments, the newly raised grenadier company, 16 guns and two petards.[7] The artillery train alone needed 16 limbers, four ball wagons, four piece wagons, 28 ammunition wagons and several materiel

---

2   Vgl.: Hassel / Vitzthum von Eckstädt, *Zur Geschichte des Türkenkrieges*, pp. 78–80, 101–103; Schuster/Francke, *Geschichte der Sächsischen Armee*, pp. 100–101.

3   Hassel / Vitzthum von Eckstädt, *Zur Geschichte des Türkenkrieges*, pp. 82–83.

4   *Ibid.*, pp. 107–108; Schuster/Francke, *Geschichte der Sächsischen Armee*, S. 101.

5   Vgl.: Schuster/Francke, *Geschichte der Sächsischen Armee*, S. 101–102; Beust, *Feldzüge*, p. 74.

6   SächsHsta DD 11237-10812/15, fol. 1.

7   Kretzschmar, *Feldartillerie*, p. 5 just mentions the 16 guns, not the petards.

wagons. The infantry was dressed in grey tunics, except for the Lifeguards, which had red ones. The Elector ordered that all pikemen should hand their weapons to the arsenal and receive muskets and *Schweinsfedern* instead.[8]

Table 11 The Saxon army on the way to Vienna 1683[9]

Regiment of horse	*Leibregiment*
Regiment of horse	*Von der Goltz*
Regiment of horse	*Trauttmansdorff*
Regiment of horse	*Plotho*
Dragoon regiment	*Graf Reuss*
Regiment of horse	*Leibgardetrabanten zu Ross*
Regiment of foot	*Von der Goltz*
Regiment of foot	*Flemming*
Regiment of foot	*Löben*
Regiment of foot	*Kuffer*
Regiment of foot	*Sachsen-Weißenfels*
Regiment of foot	*Leibregiment*
Grenadier company	*Von Bose*
Artillery	16 guns

On 28 July the army held a manoeuvre under the critical eyes of the Elector. The infantry formed two lines in the centre, the cavalry assembled on the flanks. Twenty-eight guns, which had been brought from the arsenal and were commanded by Colonel Klengel, fired a salute which was answered with three volleys from the whole army.[10]

Four days later, on 1 August early in the morning *reveille* was sounded. The troops assembled for a collective prayer and then marched out at 4:00 a.m.

34 The Saxon camp near Dresden, summer 1683. (Hessisches Staatsarchiv Marburg)

---

8 Vgl.: Schuster/Francke, *Geschichte der Sächsischen Armee*, pp. 102–103.
9 Vgl.: *Ibid.*, S. 102–103; Hassel/Vitzthum von Eckstädt, *Zur Geschichte des Türkenkrieges*, pp. 114–115.
10 Vgl.: SächsHsta DD 11237-10812/15, fol. 4–5; Schuster/Francke, *Geschichte der Sächsischen Armee*, p. 103; Schuckelt, *Die Türckische Cammer*, p. 169.

The complete army consisted of 3,194 men cavalry, 7,073 men infantry and 173 gunners for the 16 cannon. The first stop was Dohna, a small town in the south of Dresden, where John George spent the evening hunting.[11] From here the march continued in small stages of 15 to 20 kilometres per day. Two Imperial commissaries who reached the marching columns shortly behind Dohna begged the Elector to accelerate the pace. To his frustration they also informed him, that he had to take care himself for the army provisions, because Leopold I saw no possibility of supplying them. It was the first time that this issue would trouble their relationship.[12]

Every third or fourth day was used to rest the troops. From Dohna the army moved through the valleys of the eastern Erzgebirge and crossed the border with Bohemia near Teplitz. At Lobositz the cavalry was separated from the rest of the army. The troopers marched through Melnick, Český Brod, Lesetz and Neureichenau to Meißenau, where it reunited on 25 August with the infantry, which had marched through Budin, Welwarn, Prague, Poříčí, Tabor, Neuhaus, Weidhofen and Castle Horn. When the infantry reached Prague, the regiments pitched camp outside the city walls.[13] Here, John George received another somewhat smoothing letter of the Emperor, who promised to give "'very satisfaction'[14] in regard to supplies.

On the 25th the march continued early in the morning at 6:00 a.m. The regiments took the road to Meißenau, were they had to settle because of a heavy rain, because of which the soldiers were 'quite wet'.[15]

From Meißenau onwards the army marched combat ready, with ammunition handed to the individual soldiers. Two cavalry regiments formed the *avant-garde*. On 26 August the army biouvaqued near Krems on a small Danube island. On the city gates the Saxons saw the spiked heads of around 70 Ottomans.[16] On the day after the river was passed at Krems, where the War Council and a part of the court were left behind. The army joined the Bavarian troops and the regiments of the Franconian Circle near Reichersdorf on the 27 and marched to Tulln, where they met the Imperial and Polish forces the same day. All in all the relieving army now had approximately 79,000 men under its colours.[17]

When the army closed in with the Turks, nervousness increased from day to day. Already on 19 August the Imperial Colonel Schallenberg reached the Saxon camp with reports of skirmishes between his cavalry and the Turks, of which he claimed to have killed 3,000. On the 26th a growing turmoil broke out in camp. Rumours made the rounds that Kara Mustafa's troops had crossed the Danube and were attacking. In the end it turned out that the clamour started because some soldiers had caught a thief. The day after, when the Elector met with the Polish king, *Feldmarschal* Flemming stormed into the camp and reported that the Turks were plundering the Saxon baggage

11   Schuckelt, *Die Türckische Cammer*, p. 196.
12   *Ibid.*, p. 196.
13   SächsHsta DD 11237-10812/15, fol. 5–14.
14   Quot. after: Schuckelt, *Die Türckische Cammer*, p. 196.
15   Quot.: SächsHsta DD 11237-10812/15, fol. 17.
16   SächsHsta DD 11237-10812/15, fol. 22.
17   Vgl.: Schuster/Francke, *Geschichte der Sächsischen Armee*, p. 103.

35 This period engraving gives a good impression of the ferocious fighting at the walls of Vienna. (Romeyn de Hooghe (1645–1708), *Defence of the Fortifications of Vienna by Civilians, 1683*, from the Vienna Print Cycle)

train. John George jumped onto his horse and rode off. On the way back he was informed that the news was a false alarm: the Saxon guards on the baggage train had simply mistaken an alien-looking Polish horseman for the enemy.[18] In another instance, a supposed Turkish spy turned out to be an Italian beggar.[19]

In the meantime the situation in Vienna became more and more threatening. Provisions gradually ran out, and the Ottomans were able to open the first gaps in the city walls.

On 28 August King Jan III Sobiesky of Poland took over the supreme command over the relieving army. The allies agreed to march as quickly as possible in the direction of the beleaguered city and to take the route through the Vienna forest. Austrian cavalry took the lead to clear the way of Tatars, who always had a sharp eye on the Christian troops. This *avant-garde* was joined by 100 Saxon troopers of the *Flemming* Regiment under the command

---

18 Schuckelt, *Die Türckische Cammer*, pp. 170–171. Schuckelt quotes another diary. The one in SächsHsta DD 11237-10812/15, fol. 20, claims, that the elector was just in shirtsleeves and riding boots, when jumping on his horse.
19 SächsHsta DD 11237-10812/15, fol. 19.

of Lieutenant-Colonel Bronne. During one of the skirmishes John George's groom of the chamber von Haugwitz was killed.[20]

Two day later the combined army reached Dürrenberg, where it was joined by Emperor Leopold himself. While after the siege Leopold would present himself as invincible conqueror of the Turks, he was not much more than a guest with the army, which followed its march to Vienna on 31 August. The Polish troops now formed the right wing of the army, Bavarians and Franconians the centre and the Saxons and Austrians the left wing.[21] From John George's point of view it was a strange formation. While there was no possibility to take command of the right wing, where Jan Sobieski controlled his own troops, nor the right wing, where Charles of Lorraine as Imperial commander demanded the leading position for himself, there would have been the possibility to play a more dominant role in the centre, but this was not in the interest of the Bavarian Elector. So it was clear from the beginning that, no matter how bravely the Saxons fought, there would not be many laurels to win for their Elector.[22]

The Polish king gives a vivid impression of the Elector on this campaign, writing to his wife on 30 August: 'Yesterday the elector of Saxony rode with me around the troops, being in his daily red cloth; on the horse's bridles three or four spots of silver, no lackey or page, the tentlings of simple ticking, even assistance is not around him much, most of them officers.'[23]

On 1 September (or 11 September following the Gregorian calendar of the Catholics), the army reached the edge of the forest and foot of the Kahleberg. Heavy rain turned the roads into muddy quagmires. Scouts reported that the Ottomans had discovered the relief army and were also marching into the direction of the mountain. But the allies reached the top first, Flemming leading the advance guard of 6,000 Saxon troops. In front of them spread the wide Danube valley with the embattled city and the huge camp of tents of Kara Mustafa's army.[24]

The left flank of the relief army rested on the Kahlenberg. Here, in an old Camaldolese monastery, the Elector and Duke Charles took their quarters, as did the electoral infantry. Two Saxon and two Austrian guns were emplaced her also. As the sun was going down on the evening of 1 September, musket rattles could be heard, as outposts of Christians and Ottomans clashed at the foot of the Kahlenberg. Flemming brought forward three light pieces which fired on the Turkish skirmishers and repelled them.[25]

The next day Duke Charles formed the left wing in three battle lines. Five Saxon and six imperial battalions stood in the first line, eight Saxon and 10 Imperial in the second, together with four Saxon and five Imperial squadrons

---

20 Vgl.: Schuster/Francke, *Geschichte der Sächsischen Armee*, pp. 103–104; Schuckelt, *Die Türckische Cammer*, p. 171.
21 Vgl.: Schuster/Francke, *Geschichte der Sächsischen Armee*, p. 104.
22 Hassel / Vitzthum von Eckstädt, *Zur Geschichte des Türkenkrieges*, pp. 130–132.
23 Quot.: *Jan Sobieski. Briefe an die Königin*, p. 28.
24 Vgl.: Schuster/Francke, *Geschichte der Sächsischen Armee*, p. 105; Beust, *Feldzüge*, pp. 76–77.
25 Vgl.: Schuster/Francke, *Geschichte der Sächsischen Armee*, p. 105–106; Beust, *Feldzüge*, p. 77.

of cavalry. The reserve line was formed of two Saxon and Imperial battalions, three Saxon and six Imperial squadrons and some Polish troopers.[26]

Facing them was the right Ottoman wing under Kara Mustafa, which consisted mainly of Asian troops. The Turkish positions ran from Rußdorf, a small village directly on the Danube, right to the foothills of the mountain ridge, which flattens in the direction of the Vienna valley. The terrain between the two armies was hilly and streaked by many ravines, which were controlled by the Ottomans.[27]

In the early morning hours of 2 (12) September all regiments in the Christian army held an hour of prayer. Then a rocket gave the signal to advance. The left wing came into battle first, and all three battle lines marched down the Kahleberg. The Saxon artillery opened fire without effect.[28]

On the foot of the hill the Saxon infantry of the first line under the Duke of Saxe-Weißenfels clashed with the Ottomans and opened fire. The Saxons found cover behind a natural stone wall, covered with a fence. The second and third line tried to cross the Schreiberbachgrund, but met stubborn resistance from the superior Turkish troops. A fierce fight emerged. The Ottomans pinned down the Imperial infantry, which could not deploy in the small dell. In this critical situation, the five Saxon battalions of the first line marched to the right and attacked the enemy in the flank. Because of this, they themselves now offered their unprotected right to the Ottomans. General von Reuß asked the Franconian troops for support, but their commander declined because he had dissenting orders. So the Saxons brought forward their own battalions from the second and third line and stabilised their front.[29]

The Saxon infantry now increased the pressure and started to push the Ottomans back. Fortunes changed, after the Saxons had to advance into the open and the Ottomans now found cover in a sunken road. However, Flemming was able to organise a concentrated attack, pinning the Turks in their front and attacking them in the flank. The Saxons broke into the road and pushed the enemy back in disorder. They now concentrated their defence on the Rußberg, from where their artillery played havoc in the ranks of the Christians. The Duke of Coy led the first Saxon line and some Imperial battalions against this position and was able to storm the hill about 8:00 a.m. The fighting now petered out for a while, because both sides had to rearrange their lines. The dragoon regiment Graf Reuß, which had supported the charge dismounted, was brought out as pickets together with Imperial dragoons.[30]

The Ottoman centre, which mostly consisted of the elite janissaries, now had to defend itself against the slowly advancing Franco-Bavarian troops of the Christian centre and against Saxon troops coming down the slopes

26 Vgl.: Schuster/Francke, *Geschichte der Sächsischen Armee*, p. 105; Beust, *Feldzüge*, p. 75.
27 Vgl.: Schuster/Francke, *Geschichte der Sächsischen Armee*, p. 106.
28 SächsHsta DD 11237-10812/15, fol. 27.
29 Vgl.: Hassel / Vitzthum von Eckstädt, *Zur Geschichte des Türkenkrieges*, pp. 155–156; Schuster/Francke, *Geschichte der Sächsischen Armee*, pp. 106–107; Beust, *Feldzüge*, pp. 77–79.
30 Vgl.: Hassel / Vitzthum von Eckstädt, *Zur Geschichte des Türkenkrieges*, p. 157; Schuster/Francke, *Geschichte der Sächsischen Armee*, p. 107; Beust, *Feldzüge*, pp. 79-81.

36 Another period
engraving showing the
fighting at the battle of
Vienna and gives a detailed
impression of period uniform
fashion. (Romeyn de Hooghe
(1645–1708), *Battle of the
Imperials against the Turks to
Lift the Siege of Vienna*, from
the Vienna Print Cycle)

around the Grünzigbach. These had been battalions of the third line, which
now started a several-hour firefight.[31]

After the left Christian wing was rearranged, the Duke of Lorraine
continued his advance. The Austrians now tried to take Rußdorf, while the
Saxons marched against Heiligenstedt. The Saxon infantry advanced slowly,
making good use of its regimental guns. Both villages were finally taken
in bitter hand-to-hand combat, which forced Kara Mustafa to withdraw
his troops behind the Krottenbach. John George led his cavalry down
the Kahleberg and issued praise for his exhausted infantry for their brave
conduct.[32]

It was at least noon, when the Polish right wing had marched through
the rugged terrain and reached the Turkish positions. The advance guard
of 2,000 horsemen charged immediately, but was beaten back. During the
fighting, the bulk of Jan Sobieski's cavalry reached the battlefield. When
the Ottomans started a counter-charge, the King brought four German

---

31   Vgl.: Schuster/Francke, *Geschichte der Sächsischen Armee*, p. 107; Beust, *Feldzüge*, p. 82.
32   Vgl.: Hassel/Vitzthum von Eckstädt, *Zur Geschichte des Türkenkrieges*, pp. 158–160;
     Schuster/Francke, *Geschichte der Sächsischen Armee*, p. 107; Beust, *Feldzüge*, p. 82.

WIENN.

37 The Battle of Vienna.
The Saxon troops are in the
background on the left-hand
side. (The Siege of Vienna,
1683, by Justus van den
Nijpoort, 1694)

battalions, including one Saxon, to the front, which stopped the Ottomans with disciplined fire.[33]

In the meantime Charles of Lorraine assembled his generals on the Nußberg. Attended by John George, they witnessed the fighting on the right wing. The Duke finally asked if it would be wise to continue their own advance or if it would be better to give a rest to their soldiers. It was *Feldmarschall* von der Goltz, who urged that the army use its momentum and press on. At about 2:00 p.m. the left wing reopened the fight. The Saxon troops now tried to cross the Krottenbach, which succeeded after one and a half hours of bitter fighting.[34]

After the Austrians had taken the village of Döbling, Kara Mustafa retired his troops to Währing and a nearby hill, where a redoubt with six guns was erected. The Saxon troops advanced against this hill. The infantry tried to storm the redoubt, while John George charged with his cavalry against the nearby Ottoman forces. The Elector pushed forward so vigorously that for a short time he was surrounded by enemy soldiers. In the last moment he was saved by a handful of dragoons led by Lieutenant-Colonel Minckwitz. In the meantime, Saxon musketeers stormed the redoubt.[35]

After taking this important position, and so silencing the enemy guns, the Austrians were able to push the enemy out of Währing. In the meantime,

33   Vgl.: Schuster/Francke, *Geschichte der Sächsischen Armee*, p. 107; Beust, *Feldzüge*, p. 82.
34   Vgl.: Schuster/Francke, *Geschichte der Sächsischen Armee*, p. 108; Beust, *Feldzüge*, p. 83.
35   Vgl.: Hassel/Vitzthum von Eckstädt, *Zur Geschichte des Türkenkrieges*, pp. 163; Schuster/
      Francke, *Geschichte der Sächsischen Armee*, p. 108; Beust, *Feldzüge*, p. 83-84.

Jan Sobieski's cavalry was breaking the Turkish resistance on the other flank. The Ottomans started to flee from the battlefield and retired to their camp. In the early evening hours, between five and six, a bunch of horsemen, some of them Saxon dragoons, led by the young and yet unknown margrave Louis of Baden – later famous as 'Turklouis' ('Türkenlouis') – reached Vienna's Schottengate and chased off the Janissaries fighting there. The combined army now started to storm the enemy bivouac, the Saxon troops being led by General von Flemming.[36] All attempts of Kara Mustafa to build up a new line of defence failed. His army was now in complete panic and fled down the Danube.[37] When the Saxon troops stormed the Turkish camp:

> … what was left inside of the Turks was slaughtered and chased off, while poor captive Christians, who were down on their knees, were redeemed, and a huge treasure was taken as booty, albeit it can be taken for sure, that those taken by the Polish ('Polacken') on the right wing, especially in the Grand Vizier's tent and on other places, exceeded this by far …[38]

According to some other reports, at the end of the battle John George saw a group of Ottomans fleeing across a Danube island and slaying Christian slaves. The Elector charged with his Lifeguards, crossed the river and freed the slaves.[39]

38 The Battle of the Kahleberg from a period painting by an anonymous artist. Like many such paintings, the focus is on the fighting of the Polish troops. The Saxon army is on the far upper left of the painting. (*Siege and Relief of the City of Vienna in September 1683*, in the Museum of Military History, Vienna)

36   Vgl.: Friesen: Feldzüge in Morea 1685 u. 1686, S. 231.
37   Vgl.: Hassel/Vitzthum von Eckstädt, *Zur Geschichte des Türkenkrieges*, pp. 164–165; Schuster/Francke, *Geschichte der Sächsischen Armee*, p. 108. To Louis of Baden see: Oster: *Markgraf Ludwig Wilhelm von Baden*, pp. 90–91.
38   Quot.: SächsHsta DD 11237-10812/15, fol. 30.
39   Beust, *Feldzüge*, p. 85.

THE ARMY ON CAMPAIGN

39 Another depiction of the battle with medallions of the main protagonists. John George III is second from left on the lower row. (From *Der Türckische Schau-Platz eröfnet und fürgestelt in sehr vielen nach dem Leben gezeichneten Figuren* ... Eberhard Werner Happel et al., Hamburg, 1685)

By about 6:00 p.m. the battle was over. The allies, especially the Poles, started to plunder the rich Ottoman camp. On the day after, the defender of Vienna, General Count von Starhemberg, personally led Jan Sobieski, John George and the Bavarian elector Max Emanuel through the Schottengate into the city. Both electors immediately left the Polish king, who continued in triumph to the market place.[40]

On 4 September the Emperor made his entry into the city, his allies at his side. While Jan Sobieski urged following the beaten enemy, John George decided that he would leave the army. The Elector was grievously disappointed about a reputed lack of gratefulness on part of the Emperor, who did not mentioned any rewards or privileges for him. A member of the Imperial court supposedly hurt his feelings even more by saying that John George 'had done nothing more, than had been his duty.'[41] This disappointment resulted as much from ingratitude from the Imperial side, as the fact that the Elector started a campaign in a mix of chivalric thirst for action and political naivety, because he had not fixed any political or territorial claims in a treaty, before his army left Saxony.

On 5 September the electoral army broke camp and marched for Neuburg. From here, John George wrote a letter to Leopold, informing him about his decision and telling him that he regarded his duty as fulfilled. In Krems, John

---

40   Vgl.: Hassel/Vitzthum von Eckstädt, *Zur Geschichte des Türkenkrieges*, pp. 166–167; Schuster/Francke, *Geschichte der Sächsischen Armee*, p. 109.

41   Quot.: Detlef Döring, 'Johann Georg III. (1680–1691)/ Johann Georg IV. (1691–1694)', in: Frank-Lothar Kroll (ed.), *Die Herrscher Sachsens: Markgrafen, Kurfürsten, Könige (1089–1918)* (Munich: C.H. Beck, 2004), pp. 160–172, here, S. 165.

40 Period fight scene between a Christian cavalryman and a Turk (probably an auxiliary from the Balkans, according to the shape of his shield). (Engraving by Jan van Huchtenburg (1657–1733))

George left his army and went back to Dresden, together with von der Goltz und Flemming. Prince Christian of Saxe-Weißenfels was given the task of leading the troops back into the Electorate.[42]

The hasty departure of the Saxon contingent came as a surprise to the allies. Jan Sobieski, after claiming in a letter of 3 September that John George assured him he would 'go with me to the end of the world',[43] wrote to his wife on the 7th:

> The elector of Saxony and his army are already on their way back, after he had shown his chagrin and resentment plainly; to him I sent two richly bridled horses, two Turkish banners, four prisoners, two nice faience jars, and a rich veil for his wife. A captured sabre, bordered in gold his general Gultsch [von der Goltz] and those officers, who came to farewell me, a good horse.[44]

---

42 Vgl.: Hassel/Vitzthum von Eckstädt, *Zur Geschichte des Türkenkrieges*, pp. 158–160; Schuster/Francke, *Geschichte der Sächsischen Armee*, p. 109.

43 Quot.: *Jan Sobieski. Briefe an die Königin*, p. 41

44 Quot.: *Ibid.*, p. 43.

The rich booty of the campaign was displayed triumphantly in the arsenal in Dresden. Today it can be seen in the castle. It included 11 Turkish guns, including the six taken at the hill near Währingen, five magnificently decorated tents, an elephant and several camels. The electoral library received some richly ornamented Korans. The elephant died a few days afterwards in the cold mid-German autumn mist and John George's effort to establish camel rearing proved unsuccessful.[45]

During the 1683 campaign the army lost 470 dead, and about 330 sick and wounded had been left behind in Austria. Additionally, 445 horses had to be replaced.[46]

Even if his nebulous claims have not been fulfilled, in a military sense the campaign was definitely a success for the Elector and his army. Three years later the Turkish vice governor of Ofen claimed that the battle would have taken another course, 'if the king [*sic!*] from Saxony had not have fought so bravely and performed such a vigorous attack, for the others, especially the Imperial and Polish troops, they would not have asked.'[47]

7.2 Campaigns Against the Turks

John George never again took the field against the Turks. However in 1686 he sent 4,700 men for the Imperial war effort to Hungary for which he received 300,000 thalers subsidy. Under the command of *Generalleutnant* Duke Christian of Saxe Weimar and *Generalwachtmeister* von Traumannsdorff three regiments of Infantry – *Saxe-Weimar*, *Kuffer* and *Löben* – and two of cavalry – *Trautmannsdorff* and *Plotho* – were assembled. The corps left Saxony on 6 April and reached Esztergom on 3 June.[48]

From here Max Emmanuel moved his army in two columns on both sides of the Danube in the direction of the double city of Ofen and Pest. Both columns reunited in front of the latter on 17 June. The Turkish garrison already had retreated over the Pontoon bridge into Ofen (later known as Buda).[49]

The Saxon corps took part in the siege of Ofen, which was the main effort of the Imperials in this campaign. When news of an approaching relief army of 40,000 men reached the Bavarian elector, he ordered two general charges. Both were bloodily repulsed. Losses were high, especially within the officer corps. The Turkish garrisons also undertook sorties. On 24 July they attacked the troops in front of the castle, some of whom were Saxons. They were able to surprise them and nailed three cannons before they were beaten back by superior troops. However, Colonel Löben, Captain von Friesen, a lieutenant and 91 men were killed, Major General von Röbel, a lieutenant and 171 men

---

45 Schuckelt, *Die Türckische Cammer*, pp. 173–174.
46 Hassel/Vitzthum von Eckstädt, *Zur Geschichte des Türkenkrieges*, p. 160.
47 Quot.: Döring, 'Johann Georg III.', p. 165.
48 Schuster/Francke, *Geschichte der Sächsischen Armee*, pp. 110–111; Beust, *Feldzüge*, pp. 95–96
49 Schuckelt, *Die Türckische Cammer*, p. 175.

41 Period engraving which is mostly interesting because of the few details on camp life it gives in the left foreground.
(Siege of Buda, 1686, from *Historische Kernchronik*, 1690)

42 Another period engraving of the siege, also showing armed galleys on the Danube, which was a vital line of supply
for both armies. (Engraving by J. Christian Haffner)

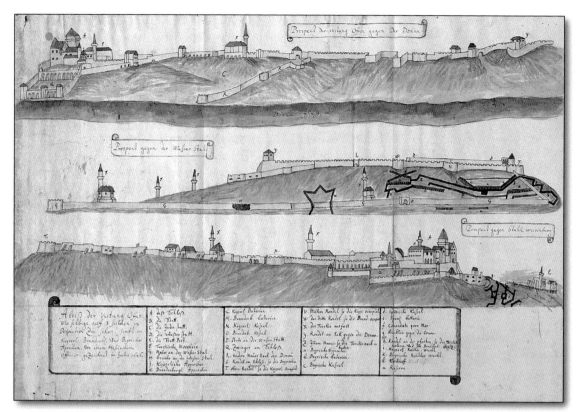

43 As this period sketch shows, that the fortifications of Ofen (Buda) were not modern, but their placement on top of a steep hill strengthened them. (Generallandesarchiv Karlsruhe)

44 Period picture showing siege batteries during the siege of Ofen (Buda) in 1686. (Date and engraver unknown)

wounded, demonstrating how eagerly this skirmish was fought. On another sortie on 11 August a further 40 Saxons were killed or wounded.[50]

Faced with the decision to raise the siege – as the Imperial army had to do two years before – Max Emmanuel instead ordered the erection of a line of contravallation. The sight of these works was impressive enough to keep the relief army of the Grand Vizier with 40,000 men (according to some reports even 60,000 men) at a distance. On 24 August Max Emanuel led a new attack on Ofen Castle with Bavarian and Saxon troops. After a pitched battle, the castle could be taken.[51]

In the meantime the Elector carefully prepared a third general charge. The heavy artillery breached day and night. The Grand Vizier's army undertook some half-hearted attacks on the siege army's camps which were all beaten back. Finally on 1 September a fresh Christian Corps of 10,000 men reached Buda, so Max Emanuel decided to storm the city the day after. This storm was conducted at 2:00 p.m. with great success but heavy losses. The Imperialists charged with 3,000 men, while a mixed force of 1,500 Bavarians, Saxons and Brandenburgians tried their luck on the other side of the city with a further 1,500 in reserve. Two more columns began feint attacks. The first charge of the Saxons and Bavarians was beaten back with heavy losses. They received 500 men as support and attacked again, taking a bastion with 16 guns. The Imperialists had also been successful. Seeing the enemy pushing into the city from all sides, the Ottomans tried to surrender. But the Christian troops, after months of deprivations, could not be stopped and massacred most of the garrison. About 3,000 were killed and 2,000 taken prisoner. In the city the victorious Christian troops found 400 guns, of which only about 170 were serviceable. The Grand Vizier burned his camp and retreated. Following the capture of Ofen the Christian army also took Szegedin and Fünfkirchen before the Saxon troops marched back home, reaching Saxony in November.[52]

In 1687 no Saxon corps was sent to Hungary, but on 17 April 1688 the Elector signed a new contract with the Emperor for providing one regiment of infantry for the ongoing war against the Ottomans. This unit was formed of detachments from all infantry regiments, making sure that no single regiment would be lost completely, but that their basic structure would be preserved. Command was assigned to Lieutenant-Colonel Cuno Christoph von Birckholz. The new unit was named *Kurprinzliches Leibregiment* which instantly attached to it an elite status.[53] On 21 April it was mustered through an Imperial commissar and taken into Imperial service. It left Saxony and marched through Bohemia and Austria to Hungary, where the Christian army under the command of the elector of Bavaria assembled around Essegg.[54] This city was taken by Max Emanuel he year before. On this occasion the

50   Beust, *Feldzüge*, p. 98.
51   *Ibid.*, p. 99.
52   Schuster/Francke, *Geschichte der Sächsischen Armee*, p. 111; Schuckelt, *Die Türckische Cammer*, pp. 175–177; Beust, *Feldzüge*, pp. 100–103.
53   Records oft he regiment and the campaign in: SächsHsta DD 10024-9130/19.
54   Schuster/Francke, *Geschichte der Sächsischen Armee*, p. 113; Beust, *Feldzüge*, pp. 104–105.

45 Tapestry in the Musée Lorrain, showing the sack of Ofen (Buda) following the siege in 1686. (Photo: Marc Baronnet. Creative Commons license CCBY-SA 4.0 <https://creativecommons.org/licenses/by-sa/4.0/deed.en>. Grayscaled)

Saxon captain Gabriel Franke captured a Janissary banner and sent it to John George III. It can still be found in the Turkish Chamber in Dresden.[55]

Although the Christian army was just 34,000 men strong – the weakest force to take the field in Hungary since 1683 – the Ottomans, having just half this number, retreated. Max Emmanuel followed them to Belgrade. The Ottoman commander Jegen Pascha left about 5,000 men behind and fled with the rest of his army, not more than 13,000. Belgrade was put under siege from 1–27 August. Forty guns and 15 mortars started a heavy bombardment, before the siege trenches were opened on the 25th. Two days later the fortress was finally taken by storm. The attackers took the outer wall and met some resistance on the inner fortifications of the city. After they broke through a massacre started, during which about 7,000 defenders and inhabitants of Belgrade were thrown to the wolves. The Saxon regiment, standing on the left of the centre, took heavy casualties on this occasion, taking 40 dead (among them two officers) and 60 wounded.[56]

After the capture of Belgrade the army – including the *Kurprinzliches Leibregiment* – took winter quarters in Hungary. Provisions were few and the

---

55   Schuckelt, *Die Türckische Cammer*, p. 177 (picture on p. 175).
56   Schuster/Francke, *Geschichte der Sächsischen Armee*, p. 113; Beust, *Feldzüge*, pp. 106–107.

46 Period engraving of the siege of Belgrade 1688. Notice the details of camp life in the foreground.
(Justus van den Nijpoort, 1694(?))

47 Period engraving showing the storm of Belgrade by Imperial troops. (Engraving by Jan Luyken, Jurraien van Poolsum, 1689)

numbers of sick rose dramatically. On 26 November von Birckholz reported 535 men able to march, 120 sick and an additional 193 sick left behind in Belgrade.[57] During the winter, the regiment was restored up to a strength of 2,000 men, the ordinary strength demanded by the Emperor for units serving in Hungary.

7.3 The Auxiliary Corps for Venice

On 28 December 1684 John George III left Dresden for Venice. He arrived at the lagoon city incognito on 25 January 1685. As Count von Hoyerswerda he took his quarter in the palace of the Comte della Thorri. However, his real identity could not be hidden for very long. Soon the rumour was on, that the famous Elector wanted to take part at the carnival. At this time Venice was bound up in a long and debilitating war with the Ottomans. The Markus Republic lacked troops. When Doge Contarini learned of the presence of the Saxon Mars, he visited him at his quarter and asked for a couple of regiments. The Republic would take over payment and rations and would also pay a remarkable sum for this help.[58]

It transpired that the actual commander of the Venetian army was a former Saxon army officer. Hannibal, Baron von Degenfeld, had left the electoral troops as colonel and now served the Serenissima as field marshal. However, John George was careful about this offer and asked his own *Feldmarschall* Flemming for advice. Flemming should also find out, which Saxon officers 'might be willing to go.'[59]

The Pomeranian was sceptical at first. In his opinion the Republic was not a reliable partner, and the troops would have been far away. Because Louis XIV was raising new troops instead of reducing his army, Flemming considered it wise to keep the army together at home. On the other hand, he recognised the argument that it would be better if the troops earn some money for the electoral chest instead of being inactive in their quarters.[60]

After this first report, which was more or less undecided about what to do, Flemming did an about turn to the pessimistic side and on 7 March sent a second report to his elector. His conclusion was that the foreign political situation was that tense, that the small Saxon army could not spare any troops. The *Feldmarschall* reminded John George that his forces had not even been able to stop the unauthorised march-through of troops from Brunswick-Lüneburg-Hannover on their way to Hungary.[61]

However, before this second report reached John George, he had signed a contract with the Republic on 8 March. The following day the electoral general adjutant von Pflug left for Dresden with orders to prepare the corps. For this, 50 men should be taken out of each infantry company. This would

---

57   SächsHsta DD 10024-9130/19, fol. 33–34.
58   Friesen, 'Feldzüge in Morea 1685 u. 1686', pp. 229–230.
59   Quot.: *Ibid.*, p. 232.
60   *Ibid.*, p. 232.
61   *Ibid.*, p. 232.

have been unfavourable for the structure of the corps, but had the advantage that after the end of the contract each Saxon infantry company would dispose a hard core of veterans. All in all 3,000 men in three regiments with 10 companies each were taken over by Venice, for which the Republic paid 120,000 thaler. It was decided that these troops should be used united and that the free religious practice of the soldiers, the majority of which have been Protestants, was guaranteed. The jurisdiction was with the regimental commanders. After the end of the contract the troops would be brought back to Venice at the cost of the Republic. There the men were to receive two months' payment before marching back to Saxony.[62]

John Georg III left Venice on 10 March and was back in Dresden on 25 April. *Feldmarschall* Flemming stuck to his critical opinion in this case, because he took an aggressive position regarding the march-through of the Hannoverian troops, which he wanted to meet with force. However, the Saxon corps was mustered by the Elector on 21 May in Pegau. It was commanded by Colonel Hans Rudolph von Schönfeld. The regiments were led by colonels Bernhard von Troppau, von Kleist and Lieutenant-Colonel von Trützschler.[63]

On 22 May the regiments started their march, after John George urgently reminded the officers 'to do their duty well, come back with honour and faithful rendered services, or never put in an appearance again.'[64]

The march through southern Germany and over the Alps was done without many difficulties. On 18 July the corps reached the Lido. It had lost so far 204 dead or deserters. The Venetian officers, who conducted the mustering of the troops, showed themselves impressed and the Duke of Brunswick-Hannover praised their appearance. After an extended time of rest, the corps was embarked on 4 August and shipped for Morea, which was reached six days later.[65]

Because the first objective of the campaign – the liberation of the harbour of Koron – was already fulfilled, the troops marched for Kalamata. Under the command of the Venetian *general capitan* Francesco Morosoni the Christian army of about 8,150 men met an Ottoman force of comparable strength. The Saxon regiments took position on the left flank. For 10 days both armies stalked each other, waiting for the enemy to make the first step or a decisive mistake. The resulting battle of Kalamata started on 14 September. The Turks vigorously attacked the left flank of Morosoni's army. Twice the Turkish cavalry charged the Saxon regiments and was beaten back with disciplined fire. Retreating to within the safe walls of the fortress, the Turks were pursued by the Saxons, which were able to storm Kalamata. Battle losses were comparably slight, the Saxons losing 21 dead and 56 wounded. A few days after the battle Morosoni wrote to the Elector: 'The brave and famous Saxon troops, which to command is my highest honour, and which vindicate the immortal glory of war of your electoral Serenity, on 14 September in front

---

62   A copy of the contract can be found in SächsHsta DD 10024-9086/11, fol. 3–5.
63   Friesen, 'Feldzüge in Morea 1685 u. 1686', pp. 234–236; Thenius, *Die Anfänge des stehenden Heerwesens*, p. 74.
64   Quot.: 'Friesen, Feldzüge in Morea 1685 u. 1686', p. 238.
65   *Ibid.*, pp. 238–242.

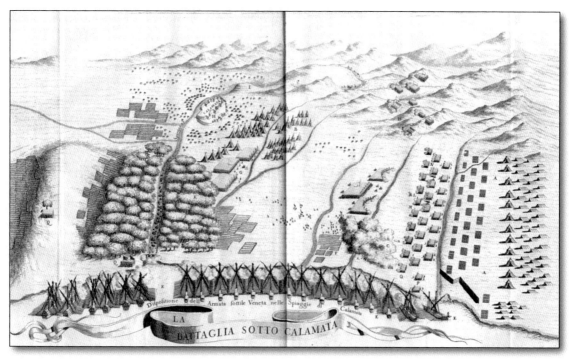

LA
BATTAGLIA SOTTO CALAMATA

48 The Battle of Kalamata. (From *Repubblica di Venezia in terra ferma*, Vincenzo Coronelli, 1688)

of the fortress Kalamata have fought most bravely against the capitain-bassa and put him into a shameful rout.'[66] These were not just eulogistics written to please John George. To a friend in Venice he wrote, that the Saxon troops 'distinguish themselves from all others by their bravery and good discipline.'[67]

Morosino followed up his victory and reconquered a number of small islands. Though the hiring contract determined the indivisibility of the corps, 900 Saxons were detached for their own expedition and later took winter quarters in Kalamata. The rest of the corps went to Corfu. The extreme climatic change of this time of the year caused many men to fall sick and soon a third of the men were in hospital.[68]

In 1686 the Ottomans started a counter-offensive and laid siege to the city of Celesa on the island of Morea, which was defended by Saxon troops. On 30 March Morosoni was able to relieve the garrison with the rest of the Saxon corps. By this time the three regiments were reduced to half their strength. The Republic requested their replenishment several times, but John George rejected them on 23 May 1686, arguing that he needed all of his troops at home. Instead he reminded the Republic, that the corps had to be given back in time the next year.[69]

The 1686 the campaign proceeded very successfully for the Venetian forces. They were able to reconquer a number of fortresses, whereby the Saxon corps was able to prove its qualities again. On 15 September Colonel

---

66   Quot.: *Ibid.*, p. 246; see also Beust, *Feldzüge*, p. 89.
67   Quot.: Friesen, 'Feldzüge in Morea 1685 u. 1686', p. 246.
68   *Ibid.*, pp. 248–250.
69   Friesen, 'Feldzüge in Morea 1685 u. 1686', pp. 250–251; Beust, *Feldzüge*, p. 90.

von Schönberg like so many of his men succumbed to a heavy sickness, while his second in command, Colonel von Kleist, had to be brought to Venice, because he suffered from consumption.[70]

In this year the artillery master (*Zeugwart*) Nestvogel and the fireworkers Demünter, Erlebach and Uhlmann travelled with the postal service to Venice. They reached Venice in April, where everybody gave a proof of his art and was taken into Venetian service. How much their work was appreciated can be seen from their high payment, Nestvogel received 100 ducats per month, the fireworkers 46. However, before they left Saxony they had to promise John George that they would return if ordered, and also that they would only work as gunners and not teach anybody in their art. In June they were shipped to Coron in Morea, which was under siege by the Venetians. On the 28th the Saxon gunners opened their fire with four heavy 500-pound mortars. The siege took several months, with a Turkish relief army nearby. Nestvogel and his men were not convinced by the way the Venetian gunners used their guns and ammunition, however they tried to force him to work their way. When Nestvogel refused, he was arrested. In his history of the Saxon field artillery Kretzschmar speculates, reasonably, that the Venetians were jealous both because of the approved superior skills of the Saxon gunners and their higher pay. Nestvogel finally asked the Venetian commander *Feldmarschal* von Degenfeldt to be relieved. But he declined this request, so the men begged their Elector for help.[71]

During the winter of 1686/87 Venice tried by all available means to extend the hiring contract. John George finally consented to it on 13 December and promised to leave his troops one more year on the Adria. The Serenissima should pay an additional 40,000 thaler. Surprisingly, the Republic declined this offer on 25 January. John George was furious and wrote a letter to the Doge on 12 February in which he demanded the immediate return of his regiments. By this time they were reduced to 1,006 men fit for service and 247 sick. Because of this the regiments were broken up and merged into one. After long delays the Saxons left the islands on 14 May and reached Venice a month later. They were quarantined for 50 days. After additional delays the regiment started its march back to Saxony. On 30 November it reached Nuremberg, where a muster revealed that the strength was further reduced to 761 men, so that a single battalion of four companies was formed. Lieutenant-Colonel von Lüttwitz, the only survivor of the three regimental commanders, took his discharge.[72]

7.4 On the Rhine Against the French

While the war against the Turks was still raging in Hungary, John George III always had a sharp eye on the western frontier of the Empire, too. Contrary to the Emperor he distrusted the irenic assurances of the Sun King and kept

---

70 Friesen, 'Feldzüge in Morea 1685 u. 1686', pp. 255–257.
71 Kretzschmar, *Feldartillerie*, pp. 141–142.
72 Vgl.: Friesen, 'Feldzüge in Morea 1685 u. 1686', S. 258–263.

his army prepared. In September 1688 the army was assembled for a grand manoeuvre near Torgau and a new *reglement* for future encampements (*Reglement wonach die Miliz bei jetzigen und künftigen campements sich zu richten*) was published. Because the old *Feldmarschall* von der Goltz at this time finally retired because of ill health, *Feldmarschallleutnant* von Flemming was promoted and officially took over the command of the army. Including the guard companies of foot and horse, the troops assembled around Torgau consisted of six regiments of foot, four of horse and one of dragoons with 19 guns, all in all about 14,900 men.[73]

Table 12 The Saxon army assembled around Torgau, September 1688. Names are of the commanding officers, not the colonel proprietors.[74]

Infantry	Cuirassier	Dragoons	Artillery
Fußtrabanten (Captain von Pflug)	Leibtrabanten (*Generalwachtmeister* von Neitschütz)	Dragonerregiment von Minckwitz (Lt. Col. Von Birkholz)	19 guns
Leibregiment (Lt. Col. Gustav Wilhelm von Schweinitz)	Leibregiment Kürassier (Lt. Col. von Trützschler)		
Feldmarschall's Regiment (Lt. Col. von der Welde)	Kürassierregiment *Haugwitz* (Lt. Col. Taler)		
Herzog Christian's Regiment (Lt. Col. Von Schmerzing)	Kürassierregiment *Bronne* (Lt. Col. Brettweiß)		
Regiment *Reuß* (Lt. Col. von der Sahla)	Kürassierregiment *Promnitz* (Lt. Col. Schachmann)		
Regiment *Zinzendorf* (Lt. Col. Röbel)			
Regiment *Kuffer* (Lt. Col. Werthmüller)			

In the second half of September a strong French army crossed the border with the Empire – without any formal declaration of war – and occupied Heidelberg, Heilbronn and even Mainz. Officially Louis XIV protected the inheritance of Liselotte von der Pfalz, daughter of Elector Charles I Louis and granddaughter of the 'winter king' Friedrich V, so that the starting war would later be known in Germany as the War of the Succession of the Palatinate (or in English-speaking regions, the Nine Years' War). The French king recognised a favourable situation, believing the Habsburgs were locked in the ongoing bitter struggle against the Ottomans.

The French threat led to several applications for help, starting with the Imperial city of Frankfurt, which were directly sent to the Elector of Saxony. In early October John George invited the new elector of Brandenburg, Frederick III, and several other princes of the Empire to a congress in Leipzig which was later moved to Magdeburg. They decided to immediately assemble

73   Beust, *Feldzüge*, p. 110.
74   Schuster/Francke, *Geschichte der Sächsischen Armee*, p. 114.

an army of 24,000 men and send it to the Rhine. John George III was willing to contribute his whole army for this campaign, Brunswick provided 7,400 men and Brandenburg another 1,500. Other small principalities provided further tiny contingents.[75]

On 3 October, even before all these arrangements were made, John George III ordered that the encampment in Torgau should be broken up by the 9th. The artillery was to be stored in the fortress, the cavalry had to move back to their old garrisons and the infantry should march for winter quarters in Thuringia, while the regiments *Reuß* and *Kuffer* marched immediately to the aid of Frankfurt.[76]

The initiative of John George and the other princes assembled in Leipzig and Magdeburg proved vital for the cause of the war, because Emperor Leopold – whom the Sun King perhaps measured correctly as phlegmatic in situations of crisis such as this – reacted very slowly with a note of protest. However, he also ordered the bigger part of the Imperial forces, which just recently had taken Belgrade from the Ottomans, back to the Empire, to support the estates of the Franconian and Swabian circles. But a march like this, over 700 miles of mostly rugged terrain with winter knocking on the doors, would prove time consuming.[77]

John George too had problems preparing his army for the new campaign, and especially raising the funds for it. The *Steuerdirektor* rejected an electoral order to transmit 310,.992 thalers to the *Kriegszahlamt*, arguing that they had not more to give than the budget calculated and confirmed by the estates for this year. It needed all of John George's electoral authority, hard words, and lots of pressure, to get this money. The Emperor published an order to all German estates, that the Saxon forces should receive 'all favourable good will and voluntary advance'.[78] However, this first order soon proved to be hollow.

On 18 October he sent his marching orders to the army which now should move in the direction of Erfurt, where the different regiments should be reassembled on the 27th. Just small garrisons for the fortresses were left behind, which in case of emergency could be filled up with the militia, which was put into a state of readiness.[79]

The artillery took a somewhat different route. Consisting of 16 guns and two petards with 92 wagons, which needed 478 horses and 237 teamsters, it was to assemble in Torgau (additional material had to be brought up from the Main Arsenal in Dresden via the Elbe), then march west to Thuringia, turn south and cross the Thuringian forest to reach the Main, from where the guns and the materiel could be shipped again in direction of Mainz. The artillery personal under the command of Lieutenant-Colonel von Borau, named Kessel, consisted of 52 men.[80]

---

75   SächsHsta DD 11237-10822/11, without fol.
76   Schuster/Francke, *Geschichte der Sächsischen Armee*, p. 115.
77   *Ibid.*, p. 115.
78   Quot.: SächsHsta DD 11237-1058, without fol.
79   Schuster/Francke, *Geschichte der Sächsischen Armee*, p. 115.
80   *Ibid.*, p. 115.

During early November John George joined his army and led the troops into the territory of Fulda. At Selnhausen the Saxons were joined by the other forces of the Magdeburg Union. The regiment *Zinzendorff* now took the lead and pushed a small French garrison out of Aschaffenburg – the first action in the new war for John George's troops.[81]

Louis XIV now sent emissaries to theElector and tried to convince him to stay neutral. John George rejected this proposal and forwarded the Sun King's letter to the Emperor, maybe to give a proof of his loyalty and so strengthen his hand for later negotiations or demands.[82]

A few days later the army entered the heavily pressed Frankfurt, saving it from the French and securing perfect winter uarters for itself, because the cold prohibited further campaigning. The Saxon army covered the south German estates in a wide arc south of the Main and east of the Rhine running from Aschaffenburg through Miltenberg up to Rothenburg ob der Tauber.[83]

The French army in this area was far superior, so John George III had to wait for the Imperial detachments which reached Franconia slowly. However, the bellicose Elector was unwilling to stay on the defensive and ordered *Generalfeldmarschal* Flemming with a corps 4,500 men to Heilbronn, an important French stronghold east of the Rhine. A French corps under the Marquis de Feuquieres had successfully invaded the country and devastated huge parts of it. Flemming moved his regiments during icy weather in the direction of the city and took the French garrison by surprise. Unprepared for a battle, the French left the city to the Saxons without any fighting. They captured a gun and 50 wagons with vital supplies.[84]

While in an operational sense the campaign so far had been another success for the Saxon elector, new quarrels started again about logistics. Emperor Leopold forwarded dozens of complaints written by the Franconian estates about the heavy charges of quartering the troops which they were encumbered with by the Saxon army. On 27 December 1688/6 January 1689 they had agreed to provide John George's troops at least with a basic provision of bread for infantry and cavalry.[85] It was the same story all over again. John George understood his contribution as part of an Imperial war and demanded the accommodation of his troops by the other estates, especially the Franconians, whom he protected from a potentially far worse treatment through the French who had already shown their brutal hand in the Palatinate. To the frustration of John George the Emperor sided with the Franconian estates and judged their complaints justifiable.[86] He even demanded that Heilbronn, which presented another place of safe winter quarters to the Saxons, should be handed over to his own troops, reaching the area in dribs and drabs. This decision provoked new letters of protest

---

81   Beust, *Feldzüge*, p. 110.
82   *Ibid.*, p. 110.
83   Schuster/Francke, *Geschichte der Sächsischen Armee*, p. 115.
84   *Ibid.*, p. 115; Beust, *Feldzüge*, p. 111.
85   SächsHsta DD 11237-10822/11, without fol.
86   The record SächsHsta DD 10024-9101/13 presents 140 letters of the Emperor, Elector and various south german estates regarding this conflict.

from the Saxon Mars, who complained that his troops, worn out in defence of the Empire, would be in want.[87]

On 1 February a new French column under the notorious Brigadier de Melac attacked the Saxon garrison at Weinheim but was repulsed with heavy casualties. Another attack on the garrison at Eich was successful and the French took 170 prisoners but left behind about 300 dead.[88]

Not all regiments were allowed to enjoy warm and cosy winter quarters. A small detachement under Lieutenant-Colonel von Schweinitz was ordered to take Diesberg am Neckar. The small town lay in the shadow of an old medieval castle and covered an important road leading from French-occupied Heidelberg into southern Germany. It took Schweinitz several weeks of fatiguing siegework in the cold winter weather, before he could take town and castle on 14 February.[89]

However strenuous the siege of the small town had been, the occupation of the mountain road put the French garrison in Heidelberg under such pressure, that they not only left the city, but also retreated back over the Rhine. On the same day the Saxons took Diesburg, the Imperial Diet in Regensburg decided to declare war on France. It took another month until this declaration was signed by the Emperor on 15 March.[90]

In the meantime the Saxon army was busy taking Rüsselsheim on the Main on 7 April. This town was just a half day's march distant from Mainz and would provide a perfect depot for the planned siege of this important Rhine fortress.[91]

All these operations had been undertaken in the absence of John George III, who spent the winter months in his comfortable residence. In early spring he left Dresden again and took his headquarters at Schweinfurt. From there he started to make preparations for a siege of Mainz, organising the Imperial forces. The Emperor begged him for some artillery, so half a dozen half-cartauns (24-pounders), a 64 and a 96-pound mortar with all equipment were transported from Dresden to the Main. On Kösen an der Saale the guns were handed to an Imperial commissary. It was agreed, that the siege train would either be handed back to the Saxons after the capture of Mainz or paid by the Emperor.[92]

By the beginning of July about 30,000 to 35,000 men, including all the Saxon troops, were assembled for the siege of Mainz. During the spring newly raised formations strengthened the Saxon forces, two new regiments of horse (*Prinz Friedrich August* and *Wolframsdorff*), a second regiment of dragoons (*Haugwitz*) and a *Freikompanie* of canoneers. The command for this prestigious operation was not handed to John George III, but to Charles of Lorraine, the victor of Vienna.[93]

---

87   Schuster/Francke, *Geschichte der Sächsischen Armee*, p. 116.
88   Beust, *Feldzüge*, p. 113.
89   Schuster/Francke, *Geschichte der Sächsischen Armee*, p. 116.
90   *Ibid.*, p. 116.
91   *Ibid.*, p. 116.
92   *Ibid.*, p. 116 A. von Kretzschmar *Feldartillerie*, p. 5.
93   Schuster/Francke, *Geschichte der Sächsischen Armee*, p. 116.

On 5 July John George III, accompanied by his two sons John George and Fredrick August, crossed the Rhine. The fortress of Mainz was situated on the western bank of the river and was now enclosed by the allied troops. A line of contravallation was erected and the Saxon troops were assigned to the right flank of it. The Elector took his headquarters at Weißenau, where the Saxons built a pontoon bridge over the Main, as did the elector of Bavaria.[94]

The siege needed eight weeks. The French garrisons started a series of sallies which were all beaten back. The Saxon troops had their share of the fighting and took serious casualties. On the 16 August a French sortie attacked the Saxon camp and was beaten back with heavy casualties, among others the general Count Reuß. In another incident Prince Frederick August, leading a column of attack, was wounded in the head. A little better aimed, and this shot could have caused serious trouble for the house of Wettin, if one remembers that the Elector and the elector prince would both die within five years, leaving Frederick August the only legitimate heir to the throne. The same was true for the Elector himself, who visited the trenches daily. On 2 August a page nearby him was killed by a cannonball which showered John George with dirt when it hit the ground.[95]

49 Duke Christian of Saxe-Weißenfels became the highest-ranking casualty in the history of the Saxon army when he fell during the siege of Mainz in 1689. (Engraving attributed to Martin Bernigeroth (1670–1733))

Frictions like this, caused by the princely thirst for glory, could have a decisive effect of the future of Europe in an age where many wars were those of succession. Frederick August was not a man to become cautious by experience. In another episode he shot off the first phalanx of his left thumb by firing a double loaded musket which exploded.[96]

On 28 August the army tried to storm the outer line of French defences. The Saxon infantry was among the first on the counterscarp but paid a heavy price in blood. *Feldmarschallieutnant* Prince Christian of Saxe-Weißenfels was killed by a musket ball, being the highest ranking casualty in Saxon military history. The army lost a further 174 dead and 1,103 wounded.[97] The day after, a French drummer beat *reveille*: the commander of Mainz, the Marquis d'Uxelles was willing to sign a capitulation. Three days later the garrison, still 8,000 men strong, left the fortress with all military honours, flags waving, drums beating and in full arms together with two mortars and six guns. They were replaced by Imperial troops. John George III received

---

94 *Ibid.*, p. 117; Beust, *Feldzüge*, p. 114.
95 Beust, *Feldzüge*, p. 118–119.
96 Georg Piltz, *August der Starke. Träume und Taten eines deutschen Fürsten* (East-Berlin: Verlag Neues Leben 1986), p. 26.
97 Beust, *Feldzüge*, p. 117.

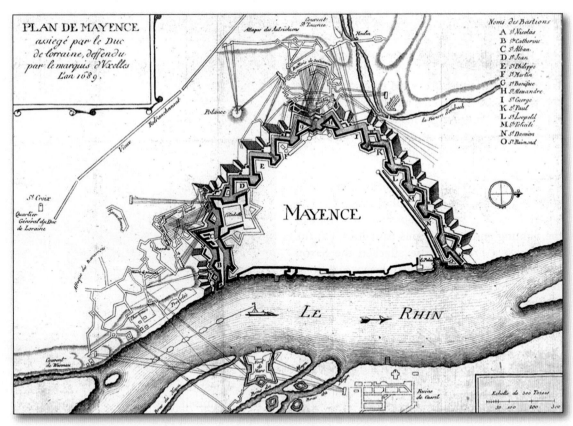

PLAN DE MAYENCE
assiégé par le Duc
de Lorraine, deffendu
par le marquis d'Vxelles
L'an 1689.

Noms des Bastions
A. St Nicolas
B. St Catherine
C. St Alban
D. St Jean
E. St Philippe
F. St Martin
G. St Boniface
H. St Alexandre
I. St George
K. St Paul
L. St Leopold
M. St Michele
N. St Damien
O. St Raimond

MAYENCE.

LE → RHIN

50 Plan of the siege of Mainz
in 1689. (Date and engraver
unknown)

a letter of congratulation from the Emperor, who honoured his personal bravery and that of his troops.[98]

While there were still two months of good campaign weather left, the allies fell out with each other over the question of winter quarters. During these quarrels the Emperor forwarded a letter of his *Feldmarschall* Count Dünewald, in which he complained about several cases of undisciplined behaviour on the part of the Saxons. Disgruntled once more John George III decided to recall his army, 'that was located on the Rhine river to the safety and for the protection of some hard-pressed Imperial estates, because on the same place no subsistence could be found.'[99] Another time the Saxon Mars had marched his troops against the common enemy of the Empire, seeking personal glory and demanding not much more than the subsistence of his troops by those to whom he was lending a helping hand, if no more substantial political gains could be won for Saxony. Again he was disappointed by Leopold. John George marched his troops to the Neckar and then split his army. He himself, the princes, the Lifeguards on horse and foot,[100] the cuirassier regiment *Friedrich August* and the infantry regiments *Reuß* and

98   Schuster/Francke, *Geschichte der Sächsischen Armee*, p. 117.
99   Quot. after: Schuster/Francke, *Geschichte der Sächsischen Armee*, p. 117.
100 Little information about this regiment can be found in the official history: Georg Freiherr von Hodenberg, *Das Königlich Sächsische 1. (Leib-) Grenadier-Regiment Nr. 100 in seinen*

Zinzendorf" marched back to Saxony which they reached in September. The rest of the army took quarters in Hanau and the electorate of Mainz.[101]

In spite of these troubles, Leopold early in 1690 asked once more for the help of Saxon troops. This time John George showed himself much more reluctant to follow the call. From the Imperial ambassador Count Glary he demanded assurances for winter quarters, but received only elusive answers in this case. The Elector stood firm, knowing that Leopold, who still had to fight a war on two fronts, was in need of experienced troops. This gave him the better bargaining position and in May the Emperor finally complied with all the electoral claims. Now John George reacted quickly and gave his regiments the order to march on 29 May. Within two weeks the army was assembled and left Saxony on 10 June, taking the road for Frankfurt am Main. It consisted of the Lifeguards of Foot, the infantry regiments *Feldmarschall, Graf Reuß, Zinzendorf, Prinz Christian von Sachsen-Zeitz* and *Uetterrodt*, the Lifeguards of Horse and another five regiments of horse, *Feldmarschall, Bronne, Friedrich August, Promnitz, Haugwitz*, the two regiments of dragoons *Minckwitz* and *Riedesel* and 16 guns which were served by 300 men. The campaign year of 1690 did not bring much fighting for the Saxons, who were once more led by the Elector himself. Reinforced by some Imperial regiments the army had to guard the fortress of Philippsburg and spent most of its time marching through the northern Black Forest. At the end of July it was decided that the Bavarian elector should invade the Franche Comté, while the Saxon army had to guard the right bank of the Rhine. But when John George marched his troops from Heilbronn to the south, a French army under the command of the Dauphin prepared its advance to Mainz, but retreated again without doing any harm to the city. He marched south and crossed the Rhine at Fort Louis, from where he invaded Württemberg with about 45,000 men. In the meantime the Saxon army united with the Bavarian troops near Ettlingen (6 September). The German princes offered battle to the Dauphin, who decided that it would be better to retreat to Strasbourg. The Saxo-Bavarian army followed him in the hope of starting a surprise attack, when he crossed the Rhine, but nothing happened.[102]

As the year came to a close, the regiments took winter quarters near Heidelberg, but nothwithstanding the promises of the Emperor, new controversy broke out about quarters and subsistence. Frustrated, John George recalled his army once more in November.[103]

With remarkable similarities the game between Dresden and Vienna repeated itself once more during the winter. While John George III at the beginning showed growing signs of frustration, Leopold played out his Imperial authority and on 21 March 1691 demanded the support of a Saxon corps again. However, John George was willing to win personal laurels, but not to be pulled over the barrel once more by a man who year after year made

---

hervorstechenden Erlebnissen und Thaten (Dresden: Verlag und Druck G. Heinrich 1892), pp. 5–6.

101 Schuster/Francke, *Geschichte der Sächsischen Armee*, p. 117; Beust, *Feldzüge*, p. 119.
102 Beust, *Feldzüge*, pp. 121–123.
103 Schuster/Francke, *Geschichte der Sächsischen Armee*, pp. 117–118.

use of this willingness at the lowest possible price, if not for free. After nine days of tough negotiation a contract (*Hauptrezeß*) was signed in Torgau on 31 March. Both parties made concessions – as they had done in the years before – but what counted most at the moment, at least for the Emperor, was John George's promise to take the field with 12,000 men and to put them onto the road as soon as possible, so that he would be able to reach Heilbronn in the middle of May. To these 12,000 the 1,500 men of the *Kurprinz* regiment had to be added, which were still under Imperial contract.[104]

Preparations for the coming campaign were delayed through a change in high command. Early in April an electoral decree informed the army that *Generalfeldmarschall* Flemming was recalled by his lord, the Elector of Brandenburg and would be replaced by Hans Adam von Schöning, who just recently had left the service of the Hohenzollern. Schöning was a very experienced and skilled soldier, however it was only natural that he needed time to get used to the procedures within the Saxon army before he could do his duties in an effective manner. He was not the Elector's first choice. John George originally intended to ask for General Chauvet, but he preferred the services of the Duchy of Brunswick-Lüneburg.[105]

Schöning's duty became even more demanding, as John George was not able to join his forces at the beginning of the campaign. For years the Elector had had problems with his health, in fact during the last two campaign seasons he was not really fit to take the field. During these spring weeks his weakened body forced him to retire for a cure to the Bohemian spa of Teplice.[106]

Because of this, Schöning stood at the head of the army which left Saxony in the first half of May. Self-assertive as he was, this would not have caused him much trouble. He now had command of the largest army Saxony had put into the field since the devastating years of the Thirty Years' War, consisting of the Trabanten Guard of horse (being company size), six regiments of foot, the grenadier battalion, six regiments of horse, two of dragoons and 20 guns, three petards and 20 musketoons for grenades with 300 artillery personnel, 87 wagons and 453 draught horses.[107]

On 8 May John George – his health not yet fully recovered – left Dresden also and took the road westwards. He was joined by parts of his court and his two sons. Taking the more difficult southern route through the hills of the Erzgebirge, the party met Count Glary in Plauen. The Imperial ambassador was able to present John George III the welcome news, that Leopold I finally had decided to give him the overall command of all Imperial forces. The Imperial corps would be assigned to him and its commander, *Feldmarschall* Count Aeneas Caprara, advised to counsel him.[108] It was a good decision made in a very bad moment, because even if John George took the field once more, his constitution did not allow him to fulfil his duties as supreme

---

104 *Ibid.*, p. 118.
105 SächsHsta DD 11237-209, fol. 88.
106 Schuster/Francke, *Geschichte der Sächsischen Armee*, p. 118.
107 *Ibid.*, p. 118.
108 *Ibid.*, p. 119.

51 Army on the March. (Engraving by Carolus Allard, date unknown, after Jan van Huchtenburg (1657–1733), Adam Frans van der Meulen (1632–1690))

commander with the same vigour as he would have done some years before. Caprara on the other hand was a man who was always willing to give advice, but had an ill understanding about the subordinate character of an adviser, that would cause much trouble in the future with the no less egocentric Schöning and also Frederick August, 'serve' him in this role.[109]

On 13 June, a month later than promised, the Saxon army reached the area of Heilbronn and concentrated two days later near the town of Wimpffen. Here a pontoon bridge spanned the Neckar which was crossed by the Saxons, who reached Schwetzingen between 19 and 22 June. Four days later, John George's regiments were joined by Imperial and Swabian troops under Caprara's command near Seckenheim. The combined forces now numbered between 24,000 and 27,000 men and faced a French army under Marshall de Lorges, who had crossed the Rhine at Philippsburg and was now entrenched in a strong position near Mannheim on the left bank of the Neckar. The Saxon army recrossed this river with the help of two pontoon bridges on 28 June and encamped around the Scharrhof, an outlying estate near Sandhofen. This forced the French on the left bank of the Rhine to retire. The Saxons – lacking additional bridging material – were

---

109 See Paul Haake, 'Die Türkenfeldzüge Augusts des Starken 1695 und 1696', in *NASG* 24 (1903), pp. 134–154. Caprara not only sabotaged Frederick August's plans, and had a decisively negative influence on the campaigns. However, his intrigues finally derailed him himself, because the Emperor replaced him with the not yet famous Prince Eugene. Because Frederick August did not take the field a third time in 1697 – he was now actively engaged in the royal elections in Poland – this had the most positive effect imaginable. Eugene took supreme command and one the spectacular victory of Zenta resulting in the peace of Carlowitz, signed in the same year.

unable to follow. They had to collect boats, barges, ferries and anything else that floated in the villages nearby to build an improvised bridge. Even as this was erected, 8,000 men under the command of the elector prince crossed it to the left bank of the Rhine to establish a bridgehead. The Saxons put 24 grenadiers into a ferry, which swam down the Neckar and into the Rhine. They found an enemy flèche on the other side of the Rhine and retreated. More grenadiers and some dragoons were put into boats and first crossed over to a small river island. Here they found the rest of a bridge from which just the planks were removed. They repaired it. In the meantime the French opened fire from the other side of the river. John George sent more dragoons forward and a lively skirmish started. The Elector called for two regiments of infantry and a grenadier battalion from the main camp. In the meantime, the advance guard crossed the river in a couple of boats. They found no enemy troops – the French retreated as soon as they saw them come – and waited for the rest of the army to follow them on 4 July. John George marched the army to Frankenthal, where it pitched camp.[110]

Three days later Colonel von Röbel with a small ship, 50 grenadiers and 200 musketeers attacked another redoubt near Helmshof. This one covered the flank of the army, which had crossed the river and was successfully stormed.[111]

52 Cavalry fight. Dutch school. (*Two Fighting Horsemen*, Jan van Huchtenburg. Date unknown)

---

110 Schuster/Francke, *Geschichte der Sächsischen Armee*, p. 119; Beust, *Feldzüge*, pp. 123–125.
111 Beust, *Feldzüge*, p. 126.

53 Another cavalry clash. While not explicity depicting Saxon troops, their equipment would not have differed much from that presented in the picture. (Copy after Jan van Huchtenburg (1657–1733), after Adam Frans van der Meulen (1632–1690))

The crossing of the Rhine was celebrated as the spectacular success of the campaign. However, it uncovered the eastern bank of the river. The French made use of the situation, crossed the Rhine in force near Philippsburg and started to plunder the nearby villages and towns. When the news of this move reached John George III he immediately decided to recross the river on 16 July. The combined army moved to Rauenberg and later on to Bretten with the French retreating before them.[112]

While the decision to defend the Imperial estates on the eastern bank seemed sensible in the face of the complex constitutional structure of the Empire, Leopold I showed himself unmet. He demanded that John George should attack the enemy vigorously and throw him back on the left bank of the Rhine. The Elector felt himself unjustly criticised by the letter and defended his action. The French river crossing forced him to follow them. Now his army was seriously weakened, because at least the half of the Saxons and the other allied troops were sick, disabling it for further campaigning. John George's health itself was worsening from day to day. In the middle of August the army pitched camp at Dürmenz.[113]

His poor state of health forced the Saxon elector to leave his army on 22 August. He went to Tübingen to put himself in the hands of good physicians. Indeed he seems to have recovered quickly and the court was in high hopes that he would soon return to the army. But the recovery appeared to have been nothing more than the last gasp of a seriously weakened body. On 12

---

112 Schuster/Francke, *Geschichte der Sächsischen Armee*, p. 119; Beust, *Feldzüge*, pp. 126–127.

113 This period is covered in a war diary, which – however – gives o nly few views on operational aspects; SächsHsta DD 10024-9297/9, see also Schuster/Francke, *Geschichte der Sächsischen Armee*, pp. 119–120.

54 John George IV followed his father as elector in 1691 but died young in 1694. (Date and artist unknown)

55 Frederick August I 'the Strong' succeeded his brother in 1694 and became king of Poland in 1697. He enlarged the army of his father and led it into the Great Northern War, where it suffered a couple of serious defeats. (Engraver P. Schenck, date unknown)

September 1691 John George III died at the age of just 44. His body was brought to Freiberg, where it was buried on 11 December in the cathedral – since the Reformation the traditional burial ground of his dynasty.[114]

Just a few days after John George's death, the Saxon army swore a new oath to his successor John George IV in the biouvac at Schweigern, close to Heilbronn. However, the poor state of the allied army and the death of its commander in fact ended the campaign season of 1691. The new elector returned home on 27 September, leaving his troops in the hands of *Generalfeldmarschall* Schöning. He was able to negotiate a contract with the Franconian estates, according to which one half of the Saxon army would march home for the winter, while the other half took winter quarters along the Neckar line.[115] The new *Feldmarschall* showed himself able to solve a problem which the old elector was never able to crack.

---

114 Beust, *Feldzüge*, p. 128.
115 SächsHsta DD 11237-463, fol. 157–160.

Conclusion

While the creation of standing forces constituted a tremendous challenge for an early modern state – as in fact it would today – there was no influence on the state-building process identified in John George III's electorate. Of course with the Secret War Council a new administrative institution was created, but it did not serve the raising of funds and supply, but their proper distribution. The funds for the army were granted to the Elector by his estates out of the annual tax revenue. No new taxes were created to pay the army. It was not before Saxony faced troubles in the Great Northern War and had to expand its forces for it, that John George's son Augustus the Strong felt forced to create the general consumption excise (*Generalkonsumtionsakzise*) as a first indirect tax and established the Secret Cabinet as a new executive organ.

The Saxon army John George created was a typical force of its time. There was nothing spectacularly different from other western and central European armies of the late seventeenth century. Of course, the infantry could be regarded as especially modern, being armed completely with muskets since the Vienna campaign of 1683, while the French or Austrian armies used the pike into the eighteenth century. However, that was not yet a major advantage, as long as the tactical doctrine just exchanged the pikemen for the *chevaux-de-fries* made up of the *Schweinsfedern*, carried by the musketeers. Remarkable is the orientation in administrative matters on the Brandenburgian model, demonstrating the good reputation the armies of the Great Elector enjoyed.

On the battlefield Saxon regiments quickly won recognition and earned a good reputation throughout Europe, as is demonstrated by the commentaries of the Polish king after the battle of Vienna or Venetian officers during the 1685/86 campaigns. These commentaries are proof of a comparably good discipline – and so amply demonstrate that the mass of documented complaints about bad behaviour in the home quarters are nothing untypical of this time – and tactical skill, learned through rigorous drill. However, the cabals about the supply of the troops when serving Emperor Leopold I at Vienna or later against the French also demonstrate impressively, that there is more about war-making than a good battlefield performance. Saxony never showed itself capable of (nor responsible for) providing rations and other supply for its troops when fighting far away from home. This had already caused much trouble, especially for the ordinary men, during the Nine Years'

War. However, as the Emperor could easily be blamed for this, these failures neither diminished the reputation of the army administration nor did they lead to reforms regarding logistics for long-range force projection. This in turn would cause many troubles in the first major war the Saxon army would have to fight for the interests of their ruler: the Great Northern War, when the regiments operated over the tremendous distances of thinly populated Poland. But this is another story to be told. In the early 1690s the battlefield victories outshone administrative weaknesses. But their shadows proved to be longer lasting.

Colour Plate Commentaries

Plate 1 Senior Officer of Cavalry *c.* 1680

For head protection he wears a Zischägge style cavalry helmet, which on occasion could be decorated with a red plume of feathers. He wears a back and breast plate complete with tassets. Under his armour he wears a thick buff coat made of moose skin lined in red wool. The coat would have been able to turn most sword cuts. Over his armour he wears a fine woven scarf to denote his status and carries his sword from a belt.

Plate 2 Infantry Officer, 1680s

The Saxon Army, like many other armies in Europe, had yet to introduce clothing regulations for officers. Contemporary portraits depict Saxon officers in a variety of colours, reds, dark blues in various shades, some almost black. All officers' uniforms are however, richly decorated with braid and lace. The officer depicted is wearing a coat based on that of Elector John George III, which is part of the Livrustkammaren (Royal Armoury Museum) Stockholm's collection. The officer wears a modest red scarf and carries his decorated épée sword on a richly embroidered baldric. In his right hand, he carries his officer's partizan, that bears the monogram of the Elector along with his coat of arms.

Plate 3 Cavalry Trooper, *c.* 1680

He wears a plainer version of the Zischägge cavalry helmet and a back and breast plate along with a long-sleeved buff coat made of elk or moose skin. The pistol is a wheel lock type, two of which would have been carried in holsters on his horse's saddle. The trooper would also have been issued with a carbine. A painting, the 'Battle of Vienna', housed at the Bundeswehr Military History Museum, in Dresden, depicts Saxon cavalry in red coats and hats.

The trumpeters are also depicted in red coats and dark green cuffs with gold and silver braid.

Plate 4 Gunner, *c.* 1680

The matross (*Gehilfe*) is holding a linstock, which was used to carry a fuse that could light the gun's primed touch hole or vent whilst keeping the gunner at a safe distance from the ignition. Over his left shoulder, he carries a powder flask. He wears a uniformed grey coat with red cuffs. The 'Battle of Vienna' painting of the Dresden Military History Museum depicts gunners in light grey coats with red cuffs and hose. The artillery officers are depicted in red uniforms with grey-blue cuffs and hose.

Plate 5 Musketeer, *Leibregiment zu Fuss*, Guards Infantry Regiment in 1680

The infantryman wears a red coat with white lined cuffs. The image is based on details in the books of W. Friedrich, *Die Uniformen der Kurfürstlich Sächsischen Armee: 1683–1763*. However, the painting 'The Battle of Vienna' housed at the Vienna Arsenal Museum depicts Saxon infantry, possibly from the Guards Regiment wearing yellow cuffs. This was maybe to differentiate between various companies or battalions, or possibly part of a new uniform introduced in the later 1680s.

Plate 6 Musketeer, Regiment *von Kuffer* in 1680

The rank and file of the regiment were issued with grey coats lined with green fabric. Underneath his coat, this musketeer wears a shirt with a basic cravat. He has been issued with a matchlock musket.

Plate 7A Musketeer, Regiment *Sachsen-Weissenfels*

He has been issued with a uniform coat of grey with yellow cuffs and hose. He is equipped with a collar of charges or bandoliers with which to serve his matchlock. He also carries a 'Swedish feather' often called a 'swine feather'. These shortened pikes were used to give musketeers increased protection against cavalry.

Plate 7B Musketeer, Regiment *von Löben*

Clothed in a light grey coat lined with blue, this musketeer has also been issued with a matchlock musket and 'Swedish feather'.

Plate 8 Saxon Colours

Information, contemporary depictions, and surviving examples of colours and flags of the Elector's army are extremely rare and difficult to source. The reconstructed colours depicted have in part been researched using *Die Uniformen der Kurfürstlich Sächsischen Armee 1683–1763* and various engravings, and paintings of the Siege and Relief of Vienna in 1683 from the museum collections of Dresden and Vienna.

1–2. Cavalry cornet of the first troop of the Lifeguards. Elector John George II was awarded the British Order of the Garter in 1678, so the banner of the 1st Troop of the Lifeguards was decorated with the image of the garter around the coat of arms of the Elector. The reverse side of the shows cipher with the motto *Sursum Deorsum*.

3. Unidentified Saxon Flag. This colour is based on a depiction seen in the art collection of the Arsenal Museum, Vienna. The cypher of the Saxon elector is mounted on an oval in a purple field.

4. Unidentified Saxon Flag. The sun of Jehovah is set on a field of red, white, yellow and blue diagonals. Based on a description in the book *Die Uniformen der Kurfürstlich Sächsischen Armee 1683–1763*.

5. Unidentified Saxon Flag. The Electoral Crown surrounded by palm leaves displaying one of the traditional emblems of the Holy Roman Empire: red crossed swords on a black and white box, mounted on a white field.

6. Unidentified Saxon Flag based on an example from the artwork collection of 'Arsenal' Museum in Vienna. A variant emblem of the Saxon elector is depicted in an oval, set on a red field.

Back Cover. A dragoon regimental guidon. A tentative reconstruction based on a depiction of a regimental colour on the 'Battle of Vienna' painting that is part of the Dresden Military Museum.

Bibliography

ASG = Archiv für Sächsische Geschichte
NASG = Neues Archiv für Sächsische Geschichte

Archive Sources

Sächsisches Hauptstaatsarchiv Dresden [SächsHsta DD]
10024 Geheimer Rat
Loc. 9086/11 Miliz Sachen betr. 1684–1687 [quot.: SächsHsta DD 10024-9086/11].
Loc. 9088/13 Kriegs Sachen 1683 – 1689 [quot.: SächsHsta DD 10024-9088/13].
Loc. 9101/6 Die Excesse der einquartirten Chur-Sächs. Miliz in dem Churfürstenthum Sachßen betr. 1685 [quot.: SächsHsta DD 10024-9101/6].
Loc. 9101/13 Von Kaierl. Mt für Churfl. Dchl: zu Sachsen verlangter Beytrag und Quartirung zu der Churfl. S: Arme'Verpflegung betr. 1689 [quot.: SächsHsta DD 10024-9101/13].
Loc. 9118/7 Acta, Was an Magazin Getreyde bewilligt, auch sonstausgeschrieben, in einigen Magazinen vorhanden, ingleichen vor die Armee erforderlich gewesen, betr. [quot.: SächsHsta DD 10024-9118/7].
Loc. 9121/2 Kriegs Verbrechen betr. 1608–96 [quot.: SächsHsta DD 10024-9121/2].
Loc. 9123/2 Verzeichniß, was das Kriegszahlamt auf die J. 1681–1688 aus der Steuer erhalten [quot.: SächsHsta DD 10024-9123/2].
Loc. 9130/19 Sachen Das Churprinzl. Sächs. Leib-Regiment betreffend Ao 1688 [quot.: SächsHsta DD 10024-9130/19].
Loc. 9297/9 Diarium des Feldzuges der sächsischen Truppen unter Johann Georg III. gegen die Franzosen 30. Juli–17. Septbr. 1690 [quot.: SächsHsta DD 10024-9297/9].
Loc. 9297/13 Churfürst Johann Georgs 3ten Feldzug Ao: 1689 [quot.: SächsHsta DD 10024-9297/13].
Loc. 9341/7 Acta Die Churfürstl: Säch?: Ordonance de ao 1686 und deren immediate Insinuation, ingl: das March Reglement de ao. 1687 betreffend [quot.: SächsHsta DD 10024-9341/7].
Loc. 13541/35 Verfügungen Kurfürst Johann Georgs III. v. Sachsen in Militärangelegenheiten [quot.: SächsHsta DD 10024-13541/35].

11237 Geheimes Kriegsratskollegium
Loc. 10809/2 Herzog Christian zu Sachß:Halla Regiment von 8 Companien zu Fuß betr. [quot.: SächsHsta DD 11237-10809/2].
Loc. 10809/4 Churf. Schweizer Leib:Guarde und deren Quartiere betr. Ao 1680 [quot.: SächsHsta DD 11237-10809/4].
Loc. 10809/7 Churf: Erste LeibRegiment zu Fuß in 5. Comp. Anno 1680 [quot.: SächsHsta DD 11237-10809/7].
Loc. 10809/11 Churf: Andere LeibRegiment zu Fuß bet. Anno 1680 [quot.: SächsHsta DD 11237-10809/11].
Loc. 10809/12 Churf: Leib Compagnie zu Roß. Anno 1680 [quot.: SächsHsta DD 11237-10809/12].
Loc. 10809/27 Churf: Sächß: Ordonance sub dato Dresden, den 26. January, Anno 1677 [quot.: SächsHsta DD 11237-10809/27].
Loc. 10812/15 Diarium über den Türkenfeldzug des Kurfürsten Johann Georg III. vom Abmarsch aus Dresden am 1. August 1683 bis zur Ankunft in Dresden am 24. September 1683 [quot.: SächsHsta DD 11237-10812/15].
Loc. 10817/14 Die HeerfahrtsWagen bey den Ambte Dresden und deren Zubehörungen betr. [zit.: SächsHsta DD 11237-10817/14].
Loc. 10822/11 Mit deutschen Fürsten und Ständen abgeschlossene Traktate und Rezesse wegen des Feldzugs gegen Frankreich [quot.: SächsHsta DD 11237-10822/11].
Loc. 207 Ordres De Beeydigung derer Garnisones und übrigen Soldatese, nach Churf. Durchl. Herzog Johann Georgen des II. höchstseel. Hintritt betr. Im August 1680 [zit.: SächsHsta DD 11237-207].
Loc. 208 Registraturen Vereydeter Kriegs Officirer de Anno 1680 biß 93 [quot.: SächsHsta DD 11237-208].
Loc. 209 Capitulationes und Bestallungen derer Generals Personen, Obristen und anderer Kriegs Officirer bey Churfl. Sächß. Milice de Anno 1680 biß 93 [quot.: SächsHsta DD 11237-209].
Loc. 210 Bestallung-Concepta derer Ober und anderen Vestungs Comandanten de Anno 1680–95 [quot.: SächsHsta DD 11237-210].
Loc. 211 Concepta Die Bestallung derer General-Kriegs Zahlmeistere derer Kriegs- und Feld Kriegs Zahlmeister auch Kriegs und Feld Kriegs Cassiers betr. [quot.: SächsHsta DD 11237-211].
Loc. 212 Reverse originalier Über ausgeantwortete Capitulat- und Bestallung de Anno 1680 biß 94 und 97 [quot.: SächsHsta DD 11237-212].

Loc. 213 Reverse bei Bestallungen von Oberofficieren, Kriegs-Commissarien, General-Auditeuren, Zeugwärtern pp. 1680–107 [quot.: SächsHsta DD 11237-213].

Loc. 214 Bestallungs Concepta Derer Ober Officiere der Churfl. S. Leib Garde-Trabanten zu Fuß. De anno 1680–1708 [quot.: SächsHsta DD 11237-214].

Loc. 215 Bestallungen Welche aufs Sr. Churf. Durchl. zu Sachsen Herzog Joh. Georgen des III Befehl der Obrist über sämtl. Artillerie Wolff Caspar von Klengel von denen bey der Artillerie u. dem Bau-Amte vormahls bestellt gewesenen Officierern u. Bedienten abgefordert. Anno 1681 [zit.: SächsHsta DD 11237-215].

Loc. 397 Spezialreskripte [quot.: SächsHsta DD 11237-397].

Loc. 463 Allerhöchste Ausschreiben, Befehliche, Mandata, Ordonnanzen, Patenta, Reglements u. Verbote, meist die Miliz angehend, im Drucke [unl.] und Originale 1682–97 [quot.: SächsHsta DD 11237-463].

Loc. 464 Gedruckte Mandata de Anno 1682 usq. 1692 Vol. 1 [zit.: SächsHsta DD 11237-464].

Loc. 878 Churf. Sächß. Regiment zu Fuß anizo unter des Obrist Lieutenant Escherts Commando Vom Octobr. 1680 biß Decemb. 81 [quot.: SächsHsta DD 11237-878].

Herzog Christiani zu Sachß. Weißenfels Regiment zu Fuß betr. de Anno 1680. 81. 82 [quot.: SächsHsta DD 11237-879].

Loc. 880 March Chur Sächß. KriegsVolcker vom Leib Regiment zu Fuß, so ihr Quartier verändern, im Jan. 1682 [quot.: SächsHsta DD 11237-880].

Loc. 883 Churf. Sächß. LeibRegiment zu Fuß betr. [quot.: SächsHsta DD 11237-883].

Loc. 884 Des Obristen zu Fuß, Herrn Moritz Kannens unterhabendes Regiment betr., Anno 1682 usq. 1695 [quot.: SächsHsta DD 11237-884].

Loc. 886 Des Obristen zu Fuß Hr. Hannsen George Adams von Löben unterhabendes Regiment betr. [quot.: SächsHsta DD 11237-886].

Loc. 887 Die Grenadiers Compagnie betr: unter Commando des Hauptmann de Boss Vom Junio 1683. 1684. 1685 [quot.: SächsHsta DD 11237-887].

Loc. 888 Churfürstl: Sächßis: Leib Garde-Trabanten zu Fuß betr. de Anno 1685 bis 1690 [quot.: SächsHsta DD 11237-888].

Loc. 935 Churf. Sächß. Regiment zu Roß unterm Grafen von Promniz betr. Vom Octobr 1680. 81. 82 [quot.: SächsHsta DD 11237-935].

Loc. 1058 March der Churf. Sächß. Armée ins Reich Anno 1688 [quot.: SächsHsta DD 11237-1058].

Loc. 1059 Memoria Vor Sr Churf. Durchl. zu Sachßen, in Dresden Geheimes Kriegs Raths Collegium, wie es in einem und anderen zu halten, als Sie mit dero Armée wieder die Crohn Frankreich im Reich marchiret, Anno 1688 [quot.: SächsHsta DD 11237-1059].

Loc. 2131 Elias Haußmann ObristWachtm. Löbnischen Reg zu Fuß betr. de Ao 1685 [quot.: SächsHsta DD 11237-2131].

Loc. 2132 Praetension Beym Dragoner Capitain von Kospoth, welche er der Compagnie schuldig verbl. [quot.: SächsHsta DD 11237-2132].

Loc. 2308 Verzeichnis, was bei Heerzügen die Ämter an Heerfahrtswagen und Mannschaft stellen müssen. Extrahiert aus den Amtsauszügen 1588 und folgende Jahre [quot.: SächsHsta DD 11237-2308].

Published Sources

Jan Sobieski. Briefe an die Königin. Feldzug und Entsatz von Wien 1683, edited and commented by Joachim Zeller (East-Berlin: Buchverlag der Morgen 1981).

Digitised Sources

Es ist Seine Churfl. Durchl. zu Sachsen/ [et]c. wegen itziger weitaussehenden und besorglichen Zeiten veranlasset worden/ Dero Militz mit einigen Regimentern zu Roß und Fuß zuverstärken ... : [Geben ... zu Dreßden/ den 28. Ianuarii, Anno 1682] / [Johann Georg/ Chur-Fürst] [quot.: Mandat über die Neuordnung des Militärwesens im Kurfürstentum Sachsen, January 1682].

Chur-Fürstlich Sächsische Erneuerte Ordinanz : Anno 1686.; [... zu Dreßden/ den 1. Martii, Anno 1686.] [quot.: Mandat 1686].

Anderweites March-Reglement: [Signatum Annaburg/ den 28. Martii, Anno 1691] [quot.: March-Reglement 1691]

Published Works

Anschütz, Heinrich, *Die Gewehr Fabrik Suhl im Hennebergischen, ihre Entstehung, Einrichtung und dermalige Zustand, nebst ausführlicher Beschreibung der Verfahrungsart bey Verfertigung der Militär und Jagd Gewehre* (Dresden: Arnoldsche Buchhandlung 1811).

Bauer, Frank, 'Zur Organisation und Struktur der kursächsischen Armee an der Wende vom 17. zum 18. Jahrhundert', *Sächsische Heimatblätter* 5 (1983), pp. 224.

Bauer, Gerhard, 'Der Anfang der Dresdner Garnison und der Beginn des stehenden Heeres in Sachsen' (1662–1830), *Dresdner Hefte* 53 (1998), pp. 4–12.

Beust, Friedrich Constantin Graf von, *Feldzüge der kursächsischen Armee, Bd. 2* (Hamburg: Wilhelm Rößler 1803).

Birk, Eberhard, 'Die Lineartaktik im Spiegel zeitgenössischer Ordnungsvorstellungen', *Militär und Gesellschaft in der Frühen Neuzeit* 16/1 (2012), pp. 7–40.

Black, Jeremy, *Beyond the Military Revolution. War in the Seventeenth-Century World* (London: Palgrave Macmillan 2011).

Bretschneider, Falk, 'Stockhaus, Festung, Waisenhaus. Orte der Einsperrung im frühneuzeitlichen Dresden', *Dresdner Hefte* 107 (2011), pp. 69–78.

Burschel, Peter, 'Die Erfindung der Desertion. Strukturprobleme in deutschen Söldnerheeren des 17. Jahrhunderts', in: Ulrich Bröcklin / Michael Sikora (eds) *Armeen und ihre Deserteure. Vernachlässigte Kapitel einer Militärgeschichte der Neuzeit* (Göttingen: Vandenhoeck & Ruprecht 1998), pp. 72–85.

Busch, Michael, 'Der Bauer als Soldat. Ein gescheitertes Konzept der Heeresaufbringung?' in Ralf Pröve (ed.) *Klio in Uniform? Probleme und Perspektiven einer modernen Militärgeschichte der Frühen Neuzeit* (Köln – Weimar – Wien: Böhlau Verlag, 1997), pp. 143–166.

Childs, John, *Warfare in the Seventeenth Century* (London: Cassel, 2001).

Costello, Vivien, and Glozier, Mathew, 'Hugenots in European Armies', in Mathias Asche a.o. (ed.), *Krieg, Militär und Migration in der Frühen Neuzeit* (Herrschaft und soziale Systeme in der Frühen Neuzeit 9) (Berlin: LIT Verlag 2008), pp. 91–104.

Dahlsen, Carl Sahrer von Sahr auf, 'Der kursächsische General der Infanterie Wostromürscky von Rockitting', in: *Archiv für sächsische Geschichte* 5 (1867), pp. 306–318.

Delbrück, Hans, *Geschichte der Kriegskunst, Bd. 4. Die Neuzeit. Vom Kriegswesen der Renaissance bis zu Napoleon* (Berlin: Verlag Georg Stilke 1920).

Dethloff, Andreas, *Das kursächsische Offizierskorps 1682–1806. Sozial-, Bildungs- und Karriereprofil einer militärischen Elite* (Hamburg: Verlag Dr. Kovac 2019).

Dietzel, Gustav, 'Zur Militärverfassung Kur Sachsens im 17. u. 18. Jahrhundert', *Archiv für die Sächsische Geschichte* 2 (1864), pp. 421–455.

Döring, Detlef, 'Johann Georg III. (1680–1691)/Johann Georg IV. (1691–1694)', in: Frank-Lothar Kroll (ed.), *Die Herrscher Sachsens: Markgrafen, Kurfürsten, Könige (1089–1918)* (Munich: C.H. Beck 2004), pp. 160–172.

Duchhardt, Heinz, *Balance of Power und Pentarchie. Internationale Beziehungen 1700–1785* (Handbuch der Internationalen Beziehungen 4) (Paderborn a.o.: Verlag Ferdinand Schoeningh 1997).

Dürichen, Johannes 'Geheimes Kabinett und Geheimer Rat unter der Regierung Augusts d. Starken in den Jahren 1704–1720. Ihre Verfassung und politische Bedeutung', in: *NASG* 51 (1930), pp. 68–134.

Fiedler, Siegfried, *Taktik und Strategie der Kabinettskriege 1650–1792* (Bonn: Bechtermünz 1986).

Forberger, Rudolf, *Die Manufaktur in Sachsen. Vom Ende des 16. bis zum Anfang des 19. Jahrhunderts* (Berlin: Akademie Verlag 1958).

Friesen, Ernst Freiherr von, 'Das 'Defensionswesen' im Kurfürstenthume Sachsen', *Archiv für die Sächsische Geschichte* 1 (1863), pp. 194–228.

Friesen, Ernst Freiherr von, 'Die Feldzüge der Sachsen in Morea während der Jahre 1685 u. 1686', *Archiv für die Sächsische Geschichte* 2 (1864), pp. 225–263.

Friedrich, Wolfgang, *Die Uniformen der kurfürstlich-sächsischen Armee*, Vol. 1 1683–1763 (Dresden: Selbstverlag des Arbeitskreises Sächsische Militärgeschichte e.V. 1997).

Göse, Frank, 'Der Blick über die Grenzen: Brandenburgische und sächsische Adlige im 16. und 17. Jahrhundert', *Sächsische Heimatblätter* 2 (1996), pp. 68–76.

Göse, Frank, 'Der Kabinettskrieg', in Dietrich Beyrau / Michael Hochgeschwender / Dieter Langewische (ed.), *Formen des Krieges. Von der Antike bis zur Gegenwart* (Krieg in der Geschichte 37) (Paderborn a.o.: Verlag Ferdinand Schoeningh 2007), pp. 121–147.

Göse, Frank, 'Die brandenburgisch-preußische Landmiliz: 'Reserve' des landesherrlichen *Miles perpetuus* oder Rudiment ständischen Selbstbewusstseins?', in Rüdiger Bergien / Ralf Pröve (eds), *Spießbürger, Patrioten, Revolutionäre. Militärische Mobilisierung und gesellschaftliche Ordnung der Neuzeit* (Göttingen: Vandenroeck und Ruprecht 2010), pp. 197–213.

Göse, Frank, 'Ressentimentgeladenheit und Rezeptionsbereitschaft: Bemerkungen zum kursächsisch-preußischen Verhältnis auf dem Gebiet der Militärgeschichte von der Mitte des 17. bis zur Mitte des 18. Jahrhunderts', in Christian Th. Müller / Matthias Rogg (ed.), *Das ist Militärgeschichte! Probleme – Projekte – Perspektiven* (Paderborn o.a.: Verlag Ferdinand Schoeningh 2013), pp. 383–398.

Göse, Frank, 'Von der "Juniorpartnerschaft" zur Gleichrangigkeit. Das brandenburgisch-sächsische Verhältnis im 16. und 17. Jahrhundert', in: Frank Göse a.o. (ed.): *Preußen und Sachsen. Szenen einer Nachbarschaft* (Dresden: Sandstein Verlag 2014), pp. 44–51.

Haake, Paul, *Generalfeldmarschall Hans Adam von Schöning* (Berlin: Gebr. Patel 1910).

Haake, Paul, 'Die Türkenfeldzüge Augusts des Starken 1695 und 1696', in *NASG* 24 (1903), pp. 134–154.

Hagen Haas, '"Denn die Bombe, wann sie fällt…" Zum Schicksal von Einwohnern belagerter Städte im absolutistischen Zeitalter', *Militär und Gesellschaft in der Frühen Neuzeit* 1 (2003), pp. 41–59.

Hanke, René, 'Bürger und Soldaten. Erfahrungen rheinischer Gemeinden mit dem Militär 1618–1714', in: Andreas Rutz (ed.), *Krieg und Kriegserfahrung im Westen des Reiches 1568–1714* (Herrschaft und soziale Systeme in der Frühen Neuzeit 20) (Göttingen: V&R unipress 2016), pp. 141–158.

Hassel, Paul and Eckstädt, Carl Friedrich Graf Vitzthum von, *Zur Geschichte des Türkenkrieges im Jahre 1683. Die Beteiligung der kursächsischen Truppen an demselben* (Dresden: Wilhelm Baensch Verlagshandlung 1883).

Helbig, Karl Gustav, 'Kurfürst Johann Georg der Dritte in seinen Beziehungen zum Kaiser und zum Reich 1682 und 1683', in: *Archiv für Sächsische Geschichte* 9 (1871), pp. 79–110.

Henshall, Nicholas, *The Myth of Absolutism: Change & Continuity in Early Modern European Monarchy* (London: Routledge, 1992).

Heyn, Oliver, *Das Militär des Fürstentums Sachsen-Hildburghausen 1680–1806* (Veröffentlichungen der Historischen Kommission für Thüringen, Kleine Reihe 47) (Köln – Weimar – Wien: Böhlau Verlag 2015).

Heyn, Oliver, 'Die Ernestiner und die Reichsdefension', in: Werner Greiling a.o. (ed.), *Die Ernestiner. Politik, Kultur und gesellschaftlicher Wandel* (Veröffentlichungen der Historischen Kommission für Thüringen, Kleine Reihe 50) (Köln – Weimar – Wien: Böhlau Verlag 2016), pp. 185–204.

Hippel, Wolfgang, *Armut, Unterschichten, Randgruppen in der Frühen Neuzeit* (Enzyklopädie Deutscher Geschichte in der Frühen Neuzeit 34) (München: Oldenbourg Verlag 2013).

Hilbert, Klaus, Lisweski, Eugen, and Richmann, Lothar, *Trag' diese Wehr zu Sachsens Ehr! Militärische Hieb- und Stichwaffen Sachsens von 1700 bis 1918. Aus dem Bestand des Militärhistorischen Museums Dresden* (Berlin: Brandenburgisches Verlagshaus 1994).

Hilbert, Klaus, *Blankwaffen aus drei Jahrhunderten. Zeugnisse sächsischer Waffengeschichte* (Berlin: Brandenburgisches Verlagshaus 1998).

Hodenberg, Georg Freiherr von, *Das Königlich Sächsische 1. (Leib-) Grenadier-Regiment Nr. 100 in seinen hervorstechenden Erlebnissen und Thaten* (Dresden: Verlag und Druck G. Heinrich 1892).

Hottenroth, Johann Edmund, *Geschichte der sächsischen Fahnen und Standarten* (Dresden: Kaufmann 1910).

Kaphahn, Fritz, 'Kurfürst und kursächsische Stände im 17. und beginnenden 18. Jahrhundert', *NASG* 43 (1922), pp. 62–79

König, Anton Balthasar, *Biographisches Lexikon aller Helden und Militairpersonen*. Band III (Berlin: Arnold Wever 1791).

Kretzschmar, A. von, *Die Geschichte der kurfürstlich und königlich sächsischen Feldartillerie von 1620–1820* (Berlin: without company 1876).

Kroener, Bernard R., 'Das Schwungrad an der Staatsmaschine', Die Bedeutung der bewaffneten Macht in der europäischen Geschichte der Frühen Neuzeit', in Bernard R. Kroener/Ralf Pröve (ed.), *Krieg und Frieden. Militär und Gesellschaft in der Frühen Neuzeit* (Paderborn a.o.: Verlag Ferdinand Schoeningh 1996), pp. 1–23.

Kroll, Stefan, *Soldaten im 18. Jahrhundert zwischen Friedensalltag und Kriegserfahrung. Lebenswelten und Kultur in der kursächsischen Armee 1728–1796* (Krieg in der Geschichte 26) (Paderborn e.a: Ferdinand Schoeningh 2006).

Krüger, Nina, *Landesherr und Landstände in Kursachsen auf den Ständeversammlungen der zweiten Hälfte des 17. Jahrhunderts* (Frankfurt a. M.: Peter Lang 2007).

Kuczynski, Jürgen, 'Der Alltag des Soldaten (1650–1810)', in Wolfram Wette (ed.), *Der Krieg des Kleinen Mannes. Eine Militärgeschichte von unten* (München: Piper 1992), pp. 68–75.

Lachmann, Manfred, *Gliederung und Garnisonen der sächsischen Armee vom Aufkommen des stehenden Heeres bis zum Ende der Monarchie* (Atlas zur Geschichte und Landeskunde von Sachsen, Beiheft zur Karte D III 3) (Leipzig – Dresden: Verlag der Sächsischen Akademie der Wissenschaften zu Leipzig und Landesvermessungsamt Sachsen 2008).

Lohsträter, Kai, '"an einer minut ein großes gelegen"', Militärische Kommunikation, Kriegsberichterstattung und Zeit vom 16. Bis zum 19. Jahrhundert', *Militär und Gesellschaft in der Frühen Neuzeit* 21 (2017), pp. 97–145.

Luh, Jürge, 'Religion und Türkenkrieg (1683–1699) – neu bewertet', in Michael Kaiser/Stefan Kroll (ed.) *Militär und Religiosität in der Frühen Neuzeit* (Herrschaft und soziale Systeme in der Frühen Neuzeit 4) (Münster: LIT Verlag 2004), pp. 193–206.

Lynn, John A., *Giant of the Grand Siècle. The French Army 1610–1715* (Cambridge: Cambridge University Press 1997).

Malettke, Klaus, *Hegemonie – Multipolares System – Gleichgewicht. Internationale Beziehungen 1648/1659 – 1713/1714* (Handbuch der Internationalen Beziehungen 3) (Paderborn et al: Verlag Ferdinand Schoeningh 2012).

Matzke, Judith, 'Außenpolitische Handlungsspielräume und Gesandtschaftswesen der Sekundogeniturfürstentümer', in Martina Schattkowsky / Manfred Wilde (ed.), *Sachsen und seine Sekundogenituren. Die Nebenlinien Weißenfels, Merseburg und Zeitz (1657–1746)* (Schriften zur Sächsischen Geschichte und Volkskunde 33) (Leipzig: Leipziger Universitätsverlag 2010), pp. 183–206.

Minckwitz, August von, 'Die wirtschaftlichen Einrichtungen namentlich die Verpflegungs- Verhältnisse bei der kursächsischen Kavallerie vom Jahre 1680 bis zum Anfang des laufenden Jahrhunderts', in: *NASG* 2 (1881), pp. 312–329.

Minckwitz, August von, 'Die Besatzung zu Dresden von der mittelalterlichen bis in die neuere Zeit', in: *NASG* 7 (1886), pp. 235–277.

Müller, Heinrich, and Kölling, Hartmut, *Europäische Hieb- und Stichwaffen* (East Berlin: Militärverlag der Deutschen Demokratischen Republik 1981).

Müller, Heinz, 'Wittenberg. Ein Überblick zum Festungsbau', in: *Burgenforschung aus Sachsen* 24 (2011), pp. 171–183.

Müller, Reinhold, and Friedrich, Wolfgang, *Die Armee Augusts des Starken. Das sächsische Heer von 1730 bis 1733* (East Berlin: Militärverlag der Deutschen Demokratischen Republik 1984).

Neefe, Konrad, 'Die Entwicklung der kur- und königl. sächsischen Infanteriemusik. Von den ältesten Zeiten bis Ende des 18. Jahrhunderts', in: *NASG* 18 (1897), pp. 109–125.

Neugebauer, Karl-Volker (ed.), *Grundkurs deutsche Militärgeschichte, Bd. 1: Die Zeit bis 1914. Vom Kriegshaufen zum Massenheer* (Munich: Oldenbourg Wissenschaftsverlag 2009).

Neugebauer, Wolfgang, 'Staat – Krieg – Kooperation. Zur Genese politischer Strukturen im 17. und 18. Jahrhundert', in: *Historisches Jahrbuch* 123 (2003), pp. 197–237.

Nowosadtko, Jutta, 'Ordnungselement oder Störfaktor? Zur Rolle stehender Heere innerhalb der frühneuzeitlichen Gesellschaft', in: Ralf Pröve (ed.), *Klio in Uniform? Probleme und Perspektiven einer modernen Militärgeschichte der Frühen Neuzeit* (Köln – Weimar – Wien: Böhlau 1997) pp. 5–34.

Nowosadtko, Jutta, 'Der Militärstand ist ein privilegierter Stand, der seine eigenen Gesetze, obrigkeitliche Ordnung und Gerichtsbarkeit hat. Die "Verstaatlichung" stehender Heere in systemtheoretischer Perspektive', in: Markus Meumann / Ralf Pröve (ed.), *Herrschaft in der Frühen Neuzeit. Umrisse eines dynamisch-kommunikativen Prozesses* (Herrschaft und soziale Systeme in der Frühen Neuzeit 2) (Münster: LIT Verlag 2004), pp. 121–141.

Nowosadtko, Jutta, *Stehendes Heer im Ständestaat. Das Zusammenleben von Militär- und Zivilbevölkerung im Fürstbistum Münster 1650 – 1803* (Paderborn e.o.: Ferdinand Schöningh 2010).

Ortenburg, Georg, *Waffen der Kabinettskriege 1650–1792* (Augsburg: Bechtermünz Verlag 1986).

Papke, Gerhard, *Von der Miliz zum stehenden Heer. Wehrwesen im Absolutismus* (Handbuch zur deutschen Militärgeschichte 1648–1939 1) (Munich: Bernard & Graefe, 1979)

Parrott, David, *Richelieu's Army. War, Government and Society in France, 1624–1642* (New York: Cambridge University Press, 2001).

Parrott, David, *The Business of War. Military Enterprise and Military Revolution in Early Modern Europe* (Cambridge: Cambridge University Press 2012).

Pepper, Simon, 'Aspects of operational art: communication, cannon and small war', in: Frank Tallett/ David J. B. Trim (ed.), *European Warfare 1350–1750* (Cambridge: Cambridge University Press 2010), pp. 1181–202

Piltz, Georg, *August der Starke. Träume und Taten eines deutschen Fürsten* (East-Berlin: Verlag Neues Leben, 1986)

Pröve, Ralf, 'Der Soldat in der "guten Bürgerstube". Das frühneuzeitliche Einquartierungssystem und die sozioökonomischen Folgen', in: Bernard R.Kroener/Ralf Pröve (ed.) *Krieg und Frieden. Militär und Gesellschaft in der Frühen Neuzeit* (Paderborn e.a.: Ferdinand Schöningh 1996), pp. 191–217.

Quaas, Gerhard, 'Aspekte der Heeresreform in der ersten Hälfte des 18. Jahrhunderts in Kursachsen und die Einquartierung auf dem Lande', in: Sächsische Heimatblätter 5 (1983), pp. 228–230.

Querengässer, Alexander, *Die Armee Augusts des Starken im Nordischen Krieg 1700–1721* (*Heere und Waffen*, 21) (Berlin: Zeughaus Verlag 2013).

Querengässer, Alexander, 'Von der Landesdefension zu den Kreisregimentern. Das kursächsische Milizwesen im Großen Nordischen Krieg 1700 bis 1716', in: *Zeitschrift für Heereskunde* 459 (2016), pp. 2–8.

Querengässer, Alexander, 'The Saxon Army in the Great Northern War', in: Steve Kling (ed.), *Great Northern War Compendium. A Special Collection of Articles by International Authors on the Great Northern War. Volume 1* (St. Louis: LLC dba THGC Publishing 2015), pp. 245–254.

Querengässer, Alexander, 'Kriegswesen und Herrschaftsbildung der Wettiner im späten Mittelalter', in: *NASG* 88 (2017), pp. 55–82.

Querengässer, Alexander, *Das kursächsische Militär im Großen Nordischen Krieg 1700–1717* (Krieg in der Geschichte 107) (Paderborn e.a.: Ferdinand Schöningh 2019).

Redlich, Fritz, *The German Military Enterpriser and his Work Force. 2 Bde.* (Vierteljahrschrift für Sozial- und Wirtschaftsgeschichte, Beiheft 47) (Wiesbaden: Franz Steiner Verlag 1964).

Redlich, Oswald, *Weltmacht des Barock. Österreich in der Zeit Kaiser Leopolds I* (Wien: R.M. Rohrer 1961).

Reichel, Maik, 'Das Testament Kurfürst Johann Georgs I. aus dem Jahre 1652 und der Weg zum "Freundbrüderlichen Hauptvergleich" 1657. Die Entstehung der Sekundogenituren Sachsen-Weißenfels, Sachsen-Merseburg und Sachsen-Zeitz', in: *Die sächsischen Wurzeln des Landes Sachsen-Anhalt und die Rolle der Sekundogenitur Sachsen-Zeitz. Protokoll des Wissenschaftlichen Kolloquiums am 26.10.1996 in Zeitz* (Beiträge zur Regional- und Landeskultur Sachsen-Anhalts 5) (Halle: Druck-Zuck GmbH 1997), pp. 19–42.

Rogers, Clifford J., 'Tactics and the face of battle', in: Frank Tallett/ David J.B. Trim (ed.), *European Warfare 1350–1750* (Cambridge: Cambridge University Press 2010), pp. 203–235.

Roberts, Michael, 'The Military Revolution, 1560–1660', in: Michael Roberts: Essays *in Swedish History* (Minneapolis: Weidenfeld & Nicolson 1967), pp. 195–225.

Salisch, Marcus von, 'Treue Deserteure. Das kursächsische Militär und der Siebenjährige Krieg (*Militärgeschichtliche Studien* 41) (München: Oldenburg 2009).

Schäfer, Gustav, *Geschichte des sächsischen Postwesens vom Ursprunge bis zum Uebergang in die Verwaltung des Norddeutschen Bundes* (Dresden: Verlag R. von Zahn 1979).

Schmidt, Hans, 'Der Einfluß der Winterquartiere auf Strategie und Kriegführung des Ancien Régime', in: *Historisches Jahrbuch* 92 (1972), pp. 77–91.

Schmidt, Hans, 'Staat und Armee im Zeitalter des "miles perpetuus"', in: Johannes Kunisch (ed.), *Staatsverfassung und Heeresverfassung in der europäischen Geschichte der frühen Neuzeit* (Historische Forschungen 28) (Berlin: Duncker & Humbolt 1986), pp. 213–248.

Schnitter, Helmut, *Volk und Landesdefension. Volksaufgebote, Defensionswerke, Landmilizen in den deutschen Territorien vom 15. bis zum 18. Jahrhundert* (East Berlin: Militärverlag der Deutschen Demokratischen Republik 1977).

Schnitter, Helmut, and Schmidt, Thomas, *Absolutismus und Heer* (Militärhistorische Studien, Neue Folge 25) East Berlin: Militärverlag der Deutschen Demokratischen Republik 1987).

Schuster, Oskar, and Francke, Friedrich August, *Geschichte der Sächsischen Armee von der Errichtung bis in die neueste Zeit. Bd. 1* (Leipzig: Duncker & Humbolt 1885).

Schöning, Kurd Wolfgang von, *Leben und Kriegstaten – Des General-Feldmarschalls Hans Adam von Schöning auf Tamsel* (Berlin: Lüderitz 1837).

Schuckelt, Holger, 'Die Rolle Sachsens in den Türkenkriegen des 16. und 17. Jahrhunderts', in: *Im Lichte des Halbmonds. Das Abendland und der türkische Orient. Ausstellungskatalog* (Dresden: Sandstein Verlag 1995), pp. 170–177.

Schuckelt, Holger, 'Die Kroatenleibgarde zu Ross des Kurfürsten Johann Georg II. von Sachsen', in: Dresdner Kunstblätter 5 (2005), pp. 320–329.

Schuckelt, Holger, *Die Türkische Cammer. Sammlung orientalischer Kunst in der kurfürstlich-sächsischen Rüstkammer Dresden* (Dresden: Sandstein Verlag 2010).

Schreiber, Georg, *Raimondo Montecuccoli. Feldherr, Schriftsteller und Kavalier* (Graz – Wien – Köln: Styria 2000).

Sennewald, Roland, *Das kursächsische Heer im Dreißigjährigen Krieg* (Berlin: Zeughaus Verlag 2013).

Sennewald, Roland, *Die kursächsischen Feldzeichen im Dreißigjährigen Krieg* (Berlin: Zeughaus Verlag 2013).

Sennewald, Roland, 'Die Schlacht bei Breitenfeld am 7./17. September 1631', in: Maik Reichel (ed.), *Pappenheim. Daran erkenn' ich meine Pappenheimer. Des Reiches Erbmarschall und General* (Wettin-Löbejün: Verlag Janos Stekovics 2014), pp. 79–89.

Thenius, Walter, *Die Anfänge des stehenden Heerwesens in Kursachsen unter Johann Georg III. und Johann Georg IV.* (Leipzig: Quelle & Meier 1912).

Vagts, Alfred, *A History of Militarism. Civilian and Military* (London: Hollies 1959).

Verlohren, Heinrich August, *Stammregister und Chronik der kur- und königlich sächsischen Armee von 1670 bis zum Beginn des 20. Jahrhundert* (Leipzig: C. Beck 1910).

Vollmer, Udo, *Deutsche Militär-Handfeuerwaffen. Heft 2 Sachsen* (Bad Saulgau: Self published 2002).

Vötsch, Jochen, 'Staatsbildung in Mitteldeutschland? Entstehung und Entwicklung der kursächsisch-albertinischen Nebenlinien', in: Martine Schattkowsky/Manfred Wilde, *Sachsen und seine Sekundogenituren. Die Nebenlinien Weißenfels, Merseburg und Zeitz (1657–1746)* (Schriften zur Sächsischen Geschichte und Volkskunde 33), Leipzig: Leipziger Universitätsverlag 2010), pp. 58–72.

Wilson, Peter H., *German Armies. War and German politics. 1648–1806* (London: UCL Press 1998).

Winnige, Norbert, 'Von der Kontribution zur Akzise. Militärfinanzierung als Movens staatlicher Steuerpolitik', in: Benhad R. Kroener / Ralf Pröve (ed.), *Krieg und Frieden. Militär und Gesellschaft in der Frühen Neuzeit* (Paderborn e.o.: Ferdinand Schöningh 1996), pp. 59–83.

Wollschläger, Thomas, '*Krieger mit Zirkel und Messlatte': Studien zur Entstehung, Entwicklung und Institutionalisierung von Ingenieurskorps und technischen Truppen in Brandenburg-Preußen und Sachsen zwischen 1648 und 1756* (Gießen: Tectum Verlag 1995).

Wollschläger, Thomas, *Die Military Revolution und der deutsche Territorialstaat. Determinanten der Staatskonsolidierung im europäischen Kontext 1670–1740* (Norderstedt: Books on Demand 2004).